POP
ART

JOHN RUBLOWSKY

PHOTOGRAPHY BY
KEN HEYMAN

Foreword by Samuel Adams Green
Director, Philadelphia Institute for Contemporary Art

BASIC BOOKS, INC.
PUBLISHERS
New York

10/31/66 Eastern 8195

Holst

SECOND PRINTING

© 1965 by John Rublowsky and Kenneth Heyman

Library of Congress Catalog Card Number: 65-16882

Manufactured in the United States of America

DESIGNED BY LORETTA LI

51515

L D

TO

BEN BIRILLO

whose uncanny and generous eye

taught me how to see

Foreword

The impact of the vivid American image encapsulated in the work of the pop artists is undeniable. Its appeal both to an excited public and to a once-frowning, now-condoning officialdom has been stunning. Today, critical accolade echoes an astonishing public acceptance, and pop art exhibits are being offered by galleries and museums everywhere. The accession to world-wide popularity of an art based on the ready-mades of an industrial society is an accomplished fact.

The evolution of pop art's façade fascination from the esoteric inner searching of abstract expressionism is traced in this book and offers a fascinating chapter in the history of art. Indeed, this movement has already made its influence felt, significantly altering the value of our esthetic. Art is no longer escape from, but an appreciation of, reality. Its examples are no longer "art works," but an expression served up with a breeziness and enthusiasm that communicate. The most terrestrial images now appeal to the most astute tastes.

Pop art's imagery is unashamedly inspired by the joys of the assembly line, and its evocation of commercial advertising reflects the mirth and joy of today's scene. The viewer is captivated by its immediacy, and the resulting participation is perfect. Art and viewer are both accessible and acceptable. Pop art celebrates reality and dismisses pretension.

The pop artists have created a Balzacian record of our era in which cliché and banality are served up with such delectation that they inspire reverence. Size is an important feature of the new art, and repetition and magnification are standard trappings. Details may be omitted, but little is left to one's imagination. The imagery is direct and simple. Choice of subject matter has also changed and need no longer involve an aura of inspiration. A unique and wonderful reality is the subject of pop art, and this reality generates its own aura.

Nor does the banality of this subject-matter indicate naïveté on the part of the artists. Assuming their traditional role in the avant-garde, the pop artists merely anticipate a new style that discovers fashion in the knowledge and appreciation of the everyday and ordinary. This style has reached into all segments of society. It may be reflected at a chic, sophisticated dinner party where table chatter offers a critique of the current rock-and-roll hits. It is a style that considers the latest Hollywood extravaganza a relief from the pretentious monotony of the ubiquitous "art" movie.

Pop art reflects the times. It is an expression of a society that puts less emphasis on breeding, formal education, and even wealth than on presentation. Movie stars, not scholars, are the heroes. It is a chic open to everyone, and qualifications for entry can be acquired as easily as learning the latest dance fad. Satisfaction comes from the acceptance of oneself and of our mechanized and impersonal world. This is an "other-directed" realm which rejects the severe introspection reflected in abstract expressionism.

Pop art represents our particular moment, reflecting this peculiar civilization in its acceptance of the mechanized and mass-produced. The pop artist revels in the beauty of the American assembly-line technique in which speed of acceptance of this year's model is also the omen of quick obsolescence.

And if, like last year's model, pop art should be exhausted tomorrow, its statement will remain as a valued expression of our time. History and nostalgia will alter and clarify our estimations. Perhaps, in retrospect, pop may come to be considered romantic—a celebration of the hot dogs enjoyed by children on family outings; an evocation of the vast spaces of our land given human personality by billboard signs; the comic books we once read; the cereal boxes on top of the refrigerator in mother's kitchen; the old American dream.

Yet, no apology is needed for this art or for its artists. Their accomplishment stands. Theirs is an art of immediacy, of brilliance, of mirth and joy. In their work, these artists face the now, the present, the today with pleasure and acceptance. They celebrate life. Tomorrow, they leave to the future.

SAMUEL ADAMS GREEN
Director
Philadelphia Institute for Contemporary Art

March 1965

Contents

The author, photographer, and publisher wish to thank the following organizations, publications, and individuals for their generous cooperation in making available photographs, color plates, and other materials without which this book could not have been.

Art in America
Art International
Irving Beck
Bianchini Gallery, New York
Ben Birillo
Richard Brown-Baker
Leo Castelli Gallery, New York
Green Gallery, New York
Sidney Janis Gallery, New York
The Jewish Museum, New York
Leon Kraushar
Leon A. Manuchin
Moderna Museet, Stockholm
Mr. and Mrs. Robert C. Scull
Show Magazine
Ileana Sonnabend Gallery, Paris
Stable Gallery, New York
Mr. and Mrs. Burton Tremaine
William S. Zierler

Except where otherwise noted, all black-and-white photography is by Ken Heyman

POP
ART

(*From left:*)
Claes Oldenburg,
Tom Wesselmann,
Roy Lichtenstein,
Jean Shrimpton,
James Rosenquist,
and Andy Warhol

The New Movement Arises

Art is made of the stuff of life. It is an expression that arises out of the unique experience of a particular time and place, reflecting the common knowledge of that era. By recognizing and then celebrating familiar truths, the artist raises them above the anarchy of chance occurrence. His insight lends them a formal reality. Herein lies the transforming power of art and the principal task of the artist. When he discovers one of these truths and succeeds in communicating its essence to others, the artist becomes a cultural force—an ornament in the crown of men.

When a group of artists working independently of one another discover similar truths at the same time, we have the makings of a new school, or movement. This is a rare event, and its occurrence marks a period of excitement and esthetic expansion. New paths are charted, and old values are restated in the light of the newly celebrated truths.

Such an event occurred in the mid-1940's, when a group of artists working in New York City brought a line of esthetic evolution to its logical conclusion. This movement, spearheaded by Jackson Pollock, Willem DeKooning, Franz Kline, Clifford Still, and others, developed into the influential abstract-expressionist school.

For almost twenty years, this movement dominated the art world, and its influence extended beyond into other areas of life. The esthetic tastes of a generation were molded by the daring and vitalizing innovations of the abstract-expressionist school. Its establishment as the dominant idiom saw America emerge as a major artistic contributor. The art center of the world shifted from Paris to New York.

Abstract expressionism represents the final stage in a line of development that began when Leonardo da Vinci urged students to seek beauty in "urine stains on a wall." The history of Western art can be traced through the steady drift toward abstraction and simplification.

By the beginnings of the twentieth century, this drift became a flood tide that reached its crest in the intensely personal projection of an inner vision achieved by the abstract-expressionist painters.

If this movement represents an end, the exhaustion of the expressive potentialities of a particular esthetic, it was also a revolutionary and liberating development. The abstract-expressionist painters created unique worlds within the limits of a canvas plane—worlds complete unto themselves without reference to any external reality. For the first time, art became preoccupied with and answered only to its own processes and means. A painting became a painting and nothing more. The contemplation of a painting became a purely sensual experience. Abstract expressionism gave art its own integrity.

The liberating influence of this school established the creative atmosphere that made the development of pop art possible. The paint can had to be tipped over before the hot dog or comic-strip panel could be considered an object for esthetic investigation. Indeed, tipping the can does not differ greatly from painting a hot dog as an esthetic gesture. The tipped can explores the esthetic possibilities of the accidental and spontaneous; the hot dog explores the possibilities of the banal and commonplace.

As a result of the abstract-expressionist experience, the limits of the canvas bounded a world that was complete unto itself. The artist is free to fill that world with whatever he chooses.

This artistic license is, however, limited by the past—by the usages of history. Just as a contemporary composer cannot write in the style of Mozart, so is the true artist prohibited from repeating the modes and styles of the past. Each generation of artists must search for an esthetic vocabulary that relates to the realities of its own world and time.

Abstract expressionism found its special vocabulary by turning within, by giving palpable expression to an interior vision that occurs only in the creative imagination of the artist. This is "sensibility painting" carried to its ultimate refinement. Personal, intense, lyrical—abstract expressionism provided the perfect idiom for expressing an esthetic truth that reflected a particular moment in time and history.

Pop art, utilizing the same artistic freedoms, represents the opposite pole of expression. Abstract expressionism was a turning within; pop art is a turning out. One was the ultimate in sensibility painting; the other is antisensibility, taking its esthetic from the brute presence of the objects it depicts. One was highly personalized; the other is depersonalized, anonymous. One was an end; the other is a beginning. Both make a major contribution to the history of art.

Taking its esthetic from the rare and the unique—as they occur in the imagination of the artist, in this case—abstract expressionism represents the aristocratic ideal in art, an ideal that has dominated Western art since the end of the Middle Ages. The pop movement, on the other hand, reflects a democratic ideal. It takes its esthetic from the commonplace and seeks those terrible beauties concealed in the vulgar and banal. It reflects a profound revolution in values whose agitating effects are being experienced throughout the world.

The movement revealed itself mainly through the work of five artists who share a common sensitivity to this shift in atmosphere and little else. Individually, their approach to art is as different as that of five men can be. Yet, their imagery is so closely related that their work is immediately identifiable as belonging to the same school.

What these artists have in common is an esthetic concern for the everyday images of our world as they occur mindlessly or through the needs of our industrial, urban, highly commercialized society. Based, as it is, on response to an external reality, the work of the pop artists remains highly individual. There are none of the stylistic similarities among the pop artists that we find in the cubist school, for example, or even among the abstract expressionists. The binding element in the pop movement is thematic. Stylistically, the artists remain worlds apart.

Roy Lichtenstein, who is notorious for his comic-strip paintings, arrived at his expression through an intellectual recognition of the esthetic possibilities of the cartoon technique. He stumbled on his imagery in the course of the routine experimentation that every artist practices.

In the direct simplicity of this medium, Lichtenstein discovered an idiom that was in harmony with his own creative bent and that expressed an important aspect of our reality. He exploited this discovery to develop his unique esthetic vocabulary. Actually, the comic strip is nothing new. It has been perfected through a fifty-year period of trial and error and is familiar to millions of people. Lichtenstein recognized the esthetic potentiality of the technique and acted on his insight.

An entirely different approach is revealed in the work of Claes Oldenburg, who has a nephew who brags to friends that his uncle makes the biggest hamburgers in the world. Oldenburg achieves his imagery through a fastidious purity of vision. By ruthless self-examination, by purging himself of everything extraneous to the visual experience, the artist has developed the rare ability to perceive the essence of an object with a minimum of social and psychological distortion.

The imagery in the work of James Rosenquist, on the other hand, is a function of a poetic, intensely personal response to the world he perceives. Rosenquist is fascinated by scale and sees in the gigantic commercial images of our time an expression of our rapidly expanding world. He has developed this natural response into a marked sensitivity to the bizarre and significant juxtapositions of scale and objects that occur in our world. His imagery speaks to us directly, reflecting both the irony and the wonder of the visual stimuli that assail us.

Still another approach to the common images of our world is revealed by the art of Andy Warhol. He arrives at his vision through an excess of sensitivity. Like a tuning fork vibrating in sympathy with invisible currents, his work explores a reality that exists below the surface of perception. Mechanical, repetitive, ominous, Warhol's imagery attempts to express the motif forces which underlie the perceivable world.

In some respects, Warhol's vision is the most daring. By using mechanical techniques, he has attempted to obliterate all personality and sensibility in his art. The artist, in Warhol's view, becomes a machine—a sensitive device for recording and transmitting the new realities as they are generated by the world.

Tom Wesselmann reveals a more traditional concern in his approach. His style emerges from a confrontation with classical "painterly" problems. Wesselmann explores the esthetics of the vulgar and impersonal as they relate to the traditional problems of composition and spatial balance.

His subject matter is the world around us and represents a hitherto-unexploited visual key. The cold efficiency of a modern kitchen or bathroom, the extravagant imagery of a billboard, the functional vista of a modern highway—these represent aspects of our reality which Wesselmann transforms into contemporary still-life, nude, and landscape paintings.

Tough and uncompromising, Wesselmann's art is perhaps the most difficult to properly assimilate. With no concession whatsoever to traditional values, he has applied the logic of painterly composition to a particularly personal and timely choice of imagery. The result is a threatening vision that exploits a despised aspect of contemporary reality.

Probably the most salient characteristic of the work of these artists is its visual strength and vitality. This is not surprising. Much of the subject matter of pop art is a commercial imagery whose visual appeal has been tested pragmatically through the years.

Consider, for example, so ordinary a commercial image as the label on a can of soup. The manufacture and distribution of this product represents an investment, in many cases, of millions of dollars. No effort is spared to make the finished product as attractive as possible. An army of graphic designers, advertising executives, company presidents, researchers contribute to the ultimate design. Together, this total represents an awesome amount of human energy and ability focused on this particular problem. The result is an image that quivers with accumulated energy—energy marshaled for the sole purpose of appealing to the consumer's eye.

What is true of the soup can is also true of the comic strip, the billboard, packages, and all the other commercial imagery that confronts us in our everyday lives. These visual elements have evolved through a process of commercial trial and error. Their appeal and visual vitality are proven. The same elements provide a portion of the subject matter of pop art and lend their vitality to the typical work of the school.

The movement that these five artists embody is an expression of our industrialized, mass-production society. It derives from our world —a projection of a twentieth-century landscape that could have been seen only in America. The school has universal appeal and validity, however, because it goes beyond mere nationalism to reflect a universal aspiration which has its most highly realized development in America.

To the extent that America is industrialized, democratic, and commercially developed, it is the vanguard of the twentieth century. These aspects of the American experience are spreading throughout the world. This expansion is by no means a placid process and goes by many names. Occasionally, it is called progress. More often, however, it is referred to as "coca colonization" or other such derogatory terms.

But Coca Cola, the supermarket, hot dogs and hamburgers, mass-produced automobiles and appliances, rock and roll, canned foods, television, central heating, ready-made clothes are the material manifestations of the encroaching twentieth century. They represent a goal that emerging nations as well as the more advanced European countries aspire to—whether this aspiration is admitted or not. The closer the goal is approached, the more intense the coca colonization, the more Americanized the society.

Certainly elements of charm and elegance are lost in the process. But who can deny that a supermarket is more efficient than even the most charming small specialty shop? And, if gracious service is rapidly disappearing from the world, so are the servers and the servile.

Pop art is the esthetic expression of this historic drift. Democratic, expansive, irreverent, brimming over with confidence and vitality, pop art accepts our world and seeks the beauties produced by this world. With the pop movement, American art becomes truly American for the first time and thus becomes universal. Avoiding the shallow and picaresque as they have been exploited by the regionalists and the "ashcan" school, pop art derives its unique vision and inspiration from the mythogenic forces generated by a new social and economic reality.

Without apology or reference to the European past, pop art boldly stakes out a new esthetic vista whose basis is the American experience. This factor lends the work of the school a presence unlike anything achieved before. Indeed, the word "European" has come to denote an esthetic flavor and approach in art that is antithetical to the pop school.

Pop art can be rude, boisterous, for it expresses the confidence and swagger of a new tradition that feels it is master of the world. This confidence is related to modern technology, to science, and to the awesome productivity of the machine.

Pop art can also be reflective, for it expresses the fears and anxieties of a world that neither understands itself nor has assimilated the telescoped experiences of a run-away century. This fear and anxiety is related to modern technology, to science, and to the awesome powers it has placed in the hands of man.

Because it is so much a manifestation of the present, pop art reflects the strengths and weaknesses of our world. These qualities—the good and the bad—have been brought into sharper focus than ever before and can be seen today as simply and directly as a figure in a Lichtenstein comic-strip painting.

Appropriately, pop art reflects another, equally important American tradition: Saturday night, when the boys have come down from the hills and are whooping it up. Like a Saturday night, pop art is festive, joyous, out for a good time with no holds barred. It expresses the artist's sheer, uninhibited delight with the extravagant imagery of our world. The voluptuous shape of a hamburger; the simplicity and directness of a comic-strip panel; the eye-stopping design on a can of soup; the naïvely surrealist vision of a billboard; the cold, gaudily efficient look of a "Hollywood" bath; the garish exuberance of a highway strip development. All visual aspects of the American scene come under the scrutiny of the pop artist's eye, and he revels, unashamedly, in their blatant appeal.

If pop art consisted of nothing more than this celebration of the banal and commonplace, that would be enough. Its exuberance and vitality alone would establish the movement as a major esthetic contribution. This aspect of pop art represents, however, merely one facet —the surface of the reality that the artists of the school have chosen to depict. In their exploration of the visual phenomena of our world, they have probed beneath the surface to reveal new possibilities of beauty and wonder.

Claes Oldenburg

(*Left:*) Roy Lichtenstein

Tom Wesselmann

(*Left:*) James Rosenquist

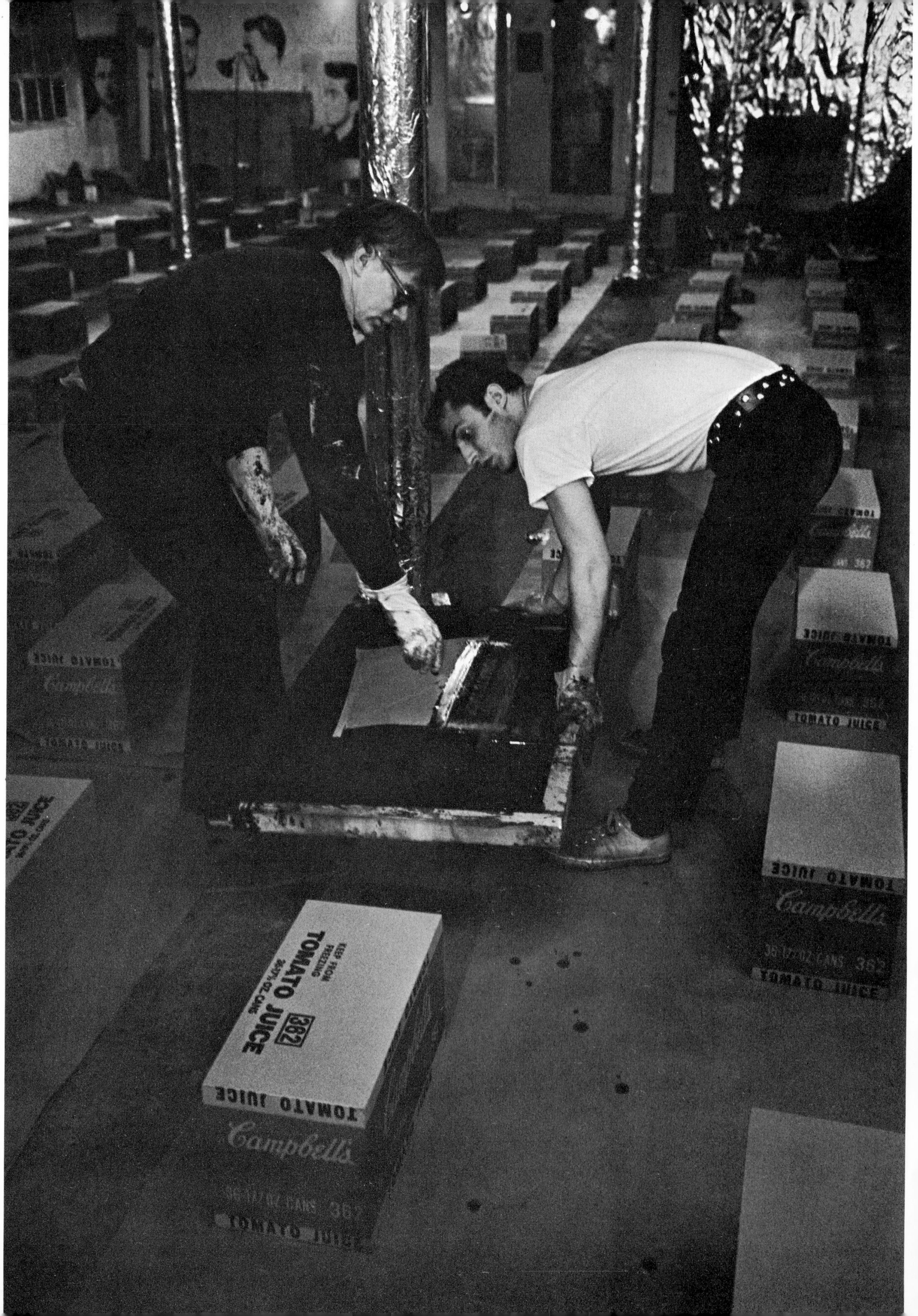
TOMATO JUICE
362
TOMATO JUICE
Campbell's

(Left:) Andy Warhol and Gerard Malanga

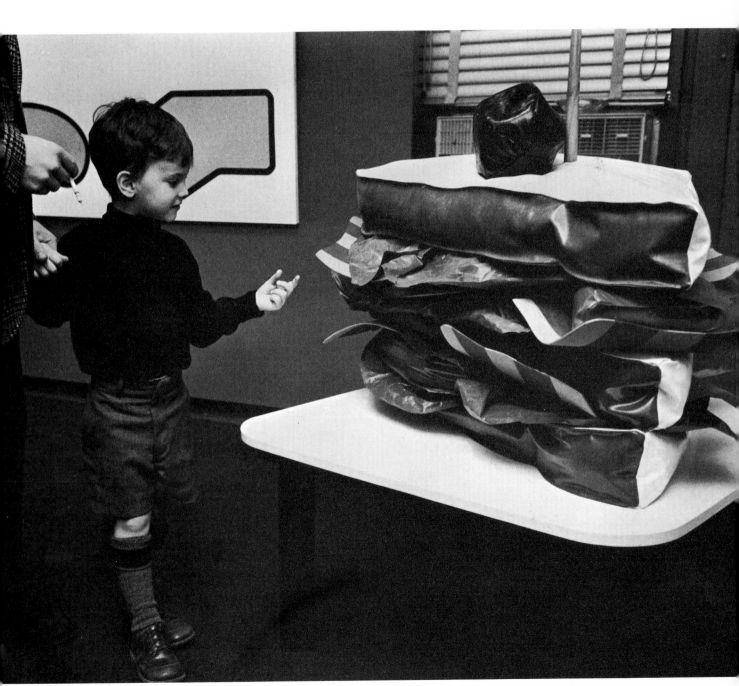

ARTS

"Bacon and Tomato Sandwich," Claes Oldenburg.
Courtesy Sidney Janis Gallery, New York.

GMX | two passenger, high performance personal automobile

"Air Hammer," James Rosenquist.
Collection Giuseppe Panza, Milan.
Photograph: Eric Pollitzer.

"Cherry Sundae," Claes Oldenburg.
Courtesy Sidney Janis Gallery, New York.
Photograph: Geoffrey Clements.

Sources

The energy that propels art forward comes from two principal sources. One of these is the immediate environment in which the artist exists and creates. In the case of such a movement as pop art, this relationship is fairly obvious. Our surroundings provide a direct thematic source for the pop artist who utilizes this material in a fundamentally realistic manner. The transforming element in pop art comes from the selectivity and sensitivity of the artist, rather than from any stylistic or painterly consideration.

The second principal source of energy is the professional milieu of the artist. This is the art world, a closely knit society full of its own intrigues and history in which the artist must find his own niche.

This art world can be likened to a multilayered pyramid whose various levels fall into constantly shifting equilibrium. The uppermost layer consists of the handful of innovators who discover and develop the dominant mode of the time. Next comes a somewhat broader level that consists of the followers. These are the artists who are directly influenced—esthetically, opportunistically, or both—by the innovations of the top strata. Below this level comes a third, rather thin, layer consisting of the mavericks—loners who absorb and impose minimum influence on the mainstreams of creation.

Finally, we come to the base of the pyramid. Here is the underworld of art—a sprawling level populated by an army of the unknown working in a ferment of creativity that exerts an explosive pressure on the layers above. Although there is a constant interaction among the various levels, the principal dynamic forces in art are generated in the underworld. When the creative ferment which characterizes this level generates sufficient pressure, it breaks through to the surface, disrupting the delicate equilibrium on all levels. When this happens, there is a major shift in the established patterns.

The top level of displaced innovators is kicked upstairs. Secure in their cultural contributions, they achieve the status of "old masters."

Thus the Jackson Pollocks become the Rembrandts. Yesterday's revolutionaries become today's pillars of tradition. The second level, that of the followers, suffers a shock. Suddenly, they discover that their mode is out of fashion, and they either attempt to adopt the new mode or they drift back into the underworld.

It is not an unfamiliar pattern. Parallels can be found in almost every human endeavor. The cycle is based on the recurring curves of creativity that accompany the growth and maturity of each new generation.

By the mid-1950's, a new equilibrium had been struck. Abstract expressionism was the undisputed master. This school had become established as the dominant artistic mode, with a substantial body of followers and a complex superstructure of galleries, museums, collectors, writers, critics, and commentators that drew on its creative energy. After years of struggle, the radical imagery and daring innovations of the movement had become accepted.

In the underworld, however, a horde of artists, powerfuly influenced by the liberating quality of abstract expressionism, were hard at work. In lofts and store fronts, alone and in cliques, young artists strained their imaginative powers to create new imageries that could challenge the established mode.

Abstract expressionism had opened the gates, and art entered an era of freedom and license such as had never been experienced before. "Anything goes!" seemed to be the motto, and art evolved out of the most unlikely areas. Young artists created accumulations of dirt and filth or they juxtaposed disjointed assortments of found objects in elaborate "combines." They created environments out of piles of old tires and explored the esthetic potentialities of pure color and random form.

Out of this creative turmoil, a few figures arose whose imagery and craft provided the leitmotiv of the future. These artists hit on thematic sources that exerted a profound influence on the rapidly developing stream of American art. They provided the first link between the abstract-expressionist experience and the subsequent development of pop art.

Richard Stankiewicz belongs among this group. A sculptor who uses the refuse of the scrap yard as his medium, he created a new kind of expression, wherein the psychological overtones of recognizable materials combined with his personal compositional feeling to project a novel esthetic aura. Full of high humor and compositional originality, his work began a tentative exploration of the esthetics of the everyday object—machinery and heavy iron components, in his case.

During the same period, Larry Rivers also began a tentative exploration of the common image in his paintings. By injecting painted objects into an abstract-expressionist field, Rivers helped bring the esthetic potentiality of the commonplace image into focus. In California, Wayne Thibaud was laying the groundwork for a peculiarly regional style of pop art. By imposing an elegant painterly style on a stark depiction of vulgar objects, he created masterful studies of pies, ice cream, and ordinary store fronts.

The esthetic of pop art was in the air, and all it needed was an additional impetus to come to realization. This thrust was provided by two remarkable artists: Robert Rauschenberg and Jasper Johns. Their work provides the bridge that links abstract expressionism and the pop movement.

In the latter half of the 1950's, Jasper Johns began work on a series of paintings that were destined to alter the course of art history. Utilizing the sensitivity and boldness of the abstract-expressionist school, Johns chose the American flag, targets, numbers, and other common images for his subject matter. Here, for the first time, this kind of visual element was used for its own sake. The common image in these paintings was neither subordinated to the over-all composition nor was it exploited for shock value. Instead, these images were merely themselves. A flag was just a flag; a number was simply a number.

The objects in these paintings take their esthetic from themselves, from their unique shapes, forms, colors, and psychological overtones. More important, however, was the fact that these paintings were successful. The imagery was fresh and strong and expressive of contemporary reality. Although the work was related to the abstract-expressionist mode, it struck out unmistakably in a direction of its own.

In many respects, this period of Jasper Johns can be considered the first expression of the pop movement. Revealed in his work is the same concern with everyday imagery. It used objects as objects and explored the expressive possibilities inherent in the vulgar and banal. At the same time, Johns's imagery was still involved with the abstract-expressionist ethos. The objects he paints are vehicles of sensibility, and he is still much concerned with personalized textures and other painterly qualities.

A close parallel can be traced between the work of Johns and Rauschenberg. While Jasper Johns was creating his flags, targets, and beer cans, using these objects to project a uniquely personal statement, Rauschenberg was utilizing real objects in his combines. By juxtaposing such diverse elements as a pillow, a stuffed eagle, a shirt, and a clock, he created a precedent-shattering concept of collage that tended to obliterate the line between art and life.

Again we have the exploitation of the common object in an expressive technique that combines the psychological aura of these real objects with the purely abstract sense of their shape, form, and texture. In Rauschenberg's combines, both these techniques work together to project a multidimensioned expression that takes its esthetic from the reality of the objects as well as from the compositional arrangement imposed on them by the artist.

The work of these two artists—Jasper Johns and Robert Rauschenberg—set the stage for the emergence of pop art. Certainly their work was familiar to the artists who were to take the next, decisive step in this line of development. Although these two artists never fully exploited the expressive potentiality of the common image, they recognized its possibilities. It was left to the next group to provide the impetus that carried pop art away from the sensibility ethos of abstract expressionism into the new esthetic.

With the work of Johns and Rauschenberg, the dike had been breached, and the new movement developed swiftly. Like a fire spreading through a tinder-dry forest, the esthetic of pop took hold. Almost simultaneously, Lichtenstein, Oldenburg, Rosenquist, Warhol, and Wesselmann revealed their individual versions of this new esthetic.

The transition was complete. Pop art was in the atmosphere, and these five artists exploited its challenging potential. On the periphery, there were such artists as James Dine, George Segal, Marisol Escobar, Robert Indiana, and others who also approached pop art. They are, however, not pop artists in the strict sense of the term. Their artistic statement, though it borrows from the reality revealed by pop art, is more closely allied to the abstract-expressionist ethos in that their statements depend on sensibility and texture for the projection of an artistic aura.

Actually, the shocking subject matter of the pop movement is not a new phenomenon in art. A similar type of imagery was arrived at by the artists of the Dada school after World War I. The Dada movement, however, rejected the accepted values of the Western world. Dadaism was antiart in that it deliberately sought out images for their shock value and for their antithetical qualities in regard to accepted standards. In the Dada experience, the imagery of the art was arbitrarily arrived at in response to a philosophic outlook. Dada art was a direct result of the application of a nihilistic ethos to the creative functions of art.

The pop movement, on the other hand, developed in response to a profound shift in esthetic atmosphere. Its imagery is a function of a new reality created by a new social and economic era. This imagery is neither meant to shock nor is it in any way antiart. It is a natural projection of the new reality created by a rapidly changing world.

The differences between Dada and pop are profound, and this difference is reflected in the work of the respective movements. But pop art owes more to abstract expressionism for its existence than it does to Dada, even though the imagery of Dada is so much closer to that of the pop movement.

In the revolutionary upheavals that characterized twentieth-century art, there were many other abortive approaches to the pop esthetic. Pablo Picasso, that fertile source of invention, created polychromed plaster statues of pastries and confections before World War I. Ferdinand Léger approached a similar idiom in his series of circus studies. Our own Stuart Davis experimented with the common image as it related to his cubist vocabulary. And, in the 1920's, Gerald Murphy, that prophetic but unappreciated American artist, did a series of paintings whose esthetic premise was almost identical with that of the pop movement today.

In all these cases, however, the tentative attempts were stillborn. They were neither fully developed nor fully exploited. Instead, they served merely as signposts for the artists of the future. The times were not propitious for this esthetic, and its development had to await a more receptive era.

This development reveals, however, the historic precedents for pop art. Startling though its imagery might be, pop art represents a logical step in the mainstream of art. The pop esthetic is neither a primitive offshoot nor a maverick development. It is a natural extension of a line of artistic development that could have come to fruition only in this particular time and place. The leaders of the pop movement gave formal reality to an esthetic truth that was already in the air.

GIRLING

GIRLING DISC BRAKES

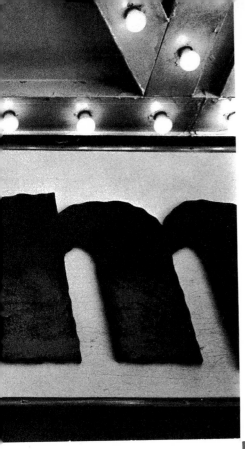

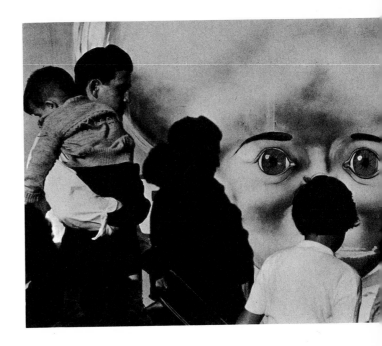

"Great American Nude Number 53,"
Tom Wesselmann.
Courtesy Green Gallery, New York.
Photograph: Rudolph Burckhardt.

"Untitled," James Rosenquist.
Collection Pasadena Art Museum.
Photograph: Rudolph Burckhardt.

PIES

"Still Life
Number 29,"
Tom Wesselmann.
*Courtesy Green
Gallery, New York.
Photograph:
Rudolph Burckhardt.*

ROY LICHTENSTEIN

Roy Lichtenstein has two sons, for whom he painted a Mickey Mouse canvas late in 1960. Fifty years from now, this story will probably be told to explain Lichtenstein's discovery of his unique imagery. His sons asked him to do a comic-strip painting and, behold, pop art! Actually, the development of Lichtenstein's style was the result of a far more complex and subtle process.

For one thing, there was no sudden, traumatic discovery. The genesis of Lichtenstein's style was spread over years, and the style is still evolving. Like every artist, Lichtenstein searched for a personalized esthetic vocabulary that could express his individuality. The ultimate resolution of this search in his now-well-known comic-strip technique occurred only gradually.

> I had been interested in the comic strip as a visual medium for a long time before I actually used it in a painting. This technique is a perfect example of an industrial process that developed as a direct result of the need for inexpensive and quick color-printing. These printed symbols attain perfection in the hands of commercial artists through the continuing idealization of the image made compatible with commercial considerations. Each generation of illustrators makes modifications and reinforcements of these symbols, which then become part of the vocabulary of all. The result is an impersonal form. In my own work, I would like to bend this toward a new classicism.

From 1951 to 1957, Lichtenstein was interested in Americana, especially of the wild West. Using the work of Remington, Ranney, and Peale as points of departure, he painted cowboys, Indians, badmen, and sheriffs in a rather cubist vein. He abandoned this tack and turned to various forms of abstract expressionism in 1957. It was about this time that he made his first few drawings of comic-strip characters. These subjects, greatly modified by an expressionist technique, occupied only a brief period, and the idea was dropped altogether, only to recur a few years later.

Again, such comic-strip characters as Bugs Bunny, Mickey Mouse, and Donald Duck were heavily disguised in an expressionist milieu. Most of these early attempts were unsuccessful, according to Lichtenstein, and were destroyed.

> When my boys asked me to paint Donald Duck, unencumbered by art, their request provided a good excuse for doing something I was already on the verge of doing at the time. My conversations with other artists and my familiarity with the work of Johns, Rauschenberg, Dine, and Oldenburg provided at least an equal impetus for the gesture.

After Lichtenstein finished this first cartoon painting, he returned briefly to the more formal idiom of abstract expressionism. He kept studying and thinking about the Donald Duck painting, however, and the more he looked at it the stronger became his conviction that he had discovered an important esthetic expression.

To test the accuracy of his initial impression, Lichtenstein did a series of seven or eight of these cartoon-type paintings. He studied them carefully. Their expressive power was undeniable. There was a mystery in the strong, direct lines of the media, and the technique lent itself to an austere simplicity of composition that the artist responded to on a very personal level.

Lichtenstein became convinced that the cartoon technique, which developed in direct response to commercial considerations, expressed something meaningful and important. They conveyed to the artist's eye the essence of our time. Lichtenstein became more and more fascinated by the expressive potentiality of the style.

The imagery of these paintings was, however, so radical, so antithetical to all accepted esthetic standards, that Lichtenstein was at first doubtful that anyone beside himself would take his work seriously. It was months before he worked up enough courage to show them to a gallery, but he did show them to close friends—fellow artists whose opinions he respected.

> I showed them to Allan Kaprow, George Segal, and Bob Watts. They were very enthusiastic about the work and recognized the same potentiality that I could discern in the medium. Allan Kaprow suggested

that I show them to the people at the Castelli Gallery who had a reputation for sympathy with new art.

Allan Kaprow made the initial introductions, and, with some anxiety, Lichtenstein made an appointment to show the paintings. Aside from a few close friends of the artist, Ivan Karp of the Castelli Gallery was the first person to see the paintings. His response was strong and immediate. Sensitive to the daring originality of the work, he asked Lichtenstein to leave the paintings.

Leo Castelli, owner of the gallery, saw the paintings the same day. His reaction was equally strong and immediate. He recognized the imagination revealed in the work and felt the power of the imagery. He agreed with Karp that the work should be shown. Later, Karp admitted that he really did not know what to make of the work. He responded to the strength and originality of the image, but the paintings were so radical, so completely new, that he could not help but question the validity of his initial judgment. He showed the work to people whose opinions he respected in order to verify his own first impression.

Among those who saw the paintings was Ben Birillo, another New York artist with a generous and uncanny eye for the new and daring. Birillo's reaction was also immediate: "These are the most terrible paintings I have ever seen," he told Karp. "You better grab the artist fast. He's great."

The unique imagery of Lichtenstein's paintings attracted the sympathetic attention of some important collectors. Richard Brown-Baker, Burton Tremaine, Phillip Johnson, David Hayes, and others responded enthusiastically to the work. On the basis of this response, the Castelli Gallery organized the first one-man show of Lichtenstein's comic-strip paintings.

The exhibition created a furor. There had not been so much excitement in the art world since the Fauvists caused riots in Paris half a century ago. Many artists were outraged and denounced Lichtenstein and the gallery while threatening to do physical damage to the paintings. People laughed at the work, and most of the established critics were spirited in their denunciations. One of them condemned Lichtenstein as "the worst artist in America."

The furor was, however, proof of the validity of Lichtenstein's vision. This kind of excitement could be generated only by significant work. The imagery was so strong that it was impossible to ignore or remain indifferent to its presence. The man responsible for the furor remained comparatively unperturbed. Lichtenstein's approach to art is professional. He knew that his paintings were radical, but he also knew that they were the result of a valid line of esthetic investigation. Success, however, made the investigation that much easier. The artist knew, now, that his work had validity in eyes other than his own.

Lichtenstein was aware that the paintings exhibited in this first one-man show were far from fully realized. They represented the first, tentative steps into a new world, and the artist had to establish his own standards and limits as he explored this new vista.

> From the beginning, I felt that the comic-strip painting had to be depersonalized. It had to express great emotions—passion, fear, violence—in an impersonal, removed, and mechanical manner. In these early paintings, there was still a good deal of personality both in the drawing and the execution. This, however, was merely the result of ineptness. I still had not learned how to use the technique with enough skill.

Gradually, the Lichtenstein image developed. The artist abandoned the stylized Donald Duck and Krazy Kat type of cartoon for the flatter and more idealized rendering of the "Romance" and "Mary Worth" style comic strip.

As his style crystallized, Lichtenstein explored the endless ramifications of the idiom. His range of subjects was almost limitless. He did a series of paintings, for example, on war—on land, sea, and air—and another on love and romance. Cliché depictions of familiar daydreams and common anxieties occupied his creative energies.

Lichtenstein's work deliberately relates to that of other artists as well as to various schools and styles. A pure explosion painting rendered in his comic-strip technique, for example, is a direct allusion to abstract expressionism. A carefully executed painting of an automobile tire, on the other hand, relates to the geometric abstractions of Vasarely, whereas the waves in such a painting as "Drowning Girl" are a direct reference to Hokusai.

The all-over pattern of his "Composition Book" alludes to the all-over paintings of Pollock and Youngerman, and Lichtenstein's cubist paintings in the cartoon manner are directly related to Picasso. Indeed, Lichtenstein also makes humorous allusions to his own work, as in the small painting which asks about his "Image Duplicator." His work explores the expressive potential of lettering, as well as combining the literary sense of words with that of the visual sense of the over-all painting.

A careful craftsman, Lichtenstein approaches his paintings in a workmanlike manner. He generally sets up a series of related paintings at the same time. The production-line method saves time and effort.

Individual paintings are usually based on comic-strip originals. Finding these models is the artist's first task. He devotes a good deal of time and effort to the search. Reading through stacks of comic books, he rarely finds more than one or two suitable models in a single book. More often, he finds none.

After choosing his models, Lichtenstein makes small pencil drawings, roughly the same size as the panel, of the principal lines of the composition. At this stage, the over-all composition is tightened, new elements added, and extraneous elements eliminated. This carefully worked-over drawing is then inserted into an enlarger which projects the image, in the size determined by the artist, onto the canvas. The lines are lightly traced. Much time is then spent restating and strengthening this drawing.

The next step is the application of the Ben Day screen—the series of regular dots that usually cover flesh tones and sky. Lichtenstein accomplishes this with the aid of a perforated metal screen and toothbrush. He had the screens made specially for him with various hole sizes. The perforated sheet is placed over the canvas, and the colored dots are brushed on through the regularly spaced holes on the screen with the toothbrush.

After the dots are applied to the canvas, Lichtenstein works on the large blocks of solid color. Though he rarely uses the same color as the model, he limits himself to the primary color palette characteristic of the comic strip. The final step is painting in the black lines. Here, again, there are considerable changes from the original.

Actually, modifications and alterations are made throughout the process. In order to divorce himself as decisively as possible from the subject matter of his paintings, Lichtenstein works on the canvases from various angles. He turns the painting upside down, on its side, diagonally, and studies the reversed image in a mirror. In this way, he is able to treat the over-all composition of his visual elements as an abstract problem in space delineation and form.

Finally, Lichtenstein studies his paintings. He leaves them in his studio for several weeks. If he is not satisfied with the impression, he makes additional changes or, when the composition does not work, he destroys the completed painting.

> Sometimes I can see that a painting is finished even before the paint dries. Other times, it takes a while before I am convinced that it is finished.

His studio is neat, but not fastidious. It is bright, airy, spacious, but not too large—just big enough for one man to work in comfortably. Everything is arranged so as to facilitate the act of painting. Brushes, paints, canvases, easels, tools—each has its own readily accessible place, but the artist is not upset when he discovers something out of place. Lichtenstein has deliberately and consciously made his studio a pleasant place in which to work.

The studio reflects the artist's professional approach to his work. This is not surprising, since Roy Lichtenstein has been painting for more than twenty years. Experience has taught him the value of order, time has impressed on him the need for discipline, and his eye and sensitivities have been sharpened by the years of constant application.

Order, discipline, eye, and sensitivity—these are the qualities that characterize and enrich Lichtenstein's work. These qualities are, however, requisites of any artist. Yet every artist does not make a major contribution to his field.

Every serious artist is confronted with a creative dilemma. He must develop an expression that does not violate his individuality, that is original and timely, that reflects a truth about reality as he perceives reality, and that can communicate the essence of that truth to others.

This combination of qualities represents an ideal that is rarely achieved. When it is, the artist makes a major contribution to the cultural record of his time. Such an opportunity is given to only a handful. Roy Lichtenstein must be included in this rare group.

"Image Duplicator,"
Roy Lichtenstein.

"Magnifying Glass,"
Roy Lichtenstein.
Courtesy Leo Castelli
Gallery, New York.
Photograph:
Rudolph Burckhardt.

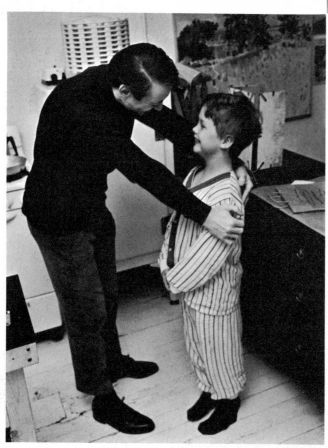

(*Right:*) Mitchell, Roy, and David Lichtenstein

CLAES OLDENBURG

Claes Oldenburg's first ambitions were literary. A graduate of Yale (class of 1950), he worked for a year and a half after graduating as a reporter and rewrite editor for the City News Bureau in Chicago. Art was relegated to the background, though Oldenburg had always been interested in painting and continued studying nights at the Chicago Art Institute.

The life of a working reporter proved, however, to be somewhat disillusioning, and early in 1952 Oldenburg abandoned the idea of a career in journalism.

> I could not see myself spending a lifetime writing meaningless reports about meaningless events. I realized that I had to do something and decided to devote myself to the ideal, rather than the practical. Art provided the means of realizing this goal, and, since I had always been interested in art, the choice seemed obvious.

Oldenburg left his job with the news bureau and enrolled at the Art Institute as a full-time student. For the next two years, he studied at the Institute while supporting himself with various part-time jobs. During one of his terms at the Institute, he worked next to H. C. Westermann, a fellow-student. Oldenburg recalls that the ideas and approach of this highly original artist acted as a catalyst on his own ideas and development.

Oldenburg was awarded a scholarship to the Saugatuck Summer School of Painting and spent the summer of 1953 at the school in Saugatuck, Michigan. Here he met Pat Muchinski, an art student from Milwaukee, whom he was to marry some seven years later in New York City.

In Chicago, Oldenburg continued working at the Institute until the fall of 1954, when he spent six months in California. This marked the end of Oldenburg's formal training. After his California visit, he returned to Chicago and worked on his own. For the next two years, he lived in a studio on North Avenue, where he experimented with various styles while developing the techniques and ideas that were to become basic to his later work. During most of this time, Oldenburg was employed by a publication called *The Chicago Magazine*. He edited the art column, designed layouts, illustrated stories, and solicited manuscripts. Finally Oldenburg came to New York early in 1956.

> I felt that I had exhausted the Chicago atmosphere as far as my work was concerned. I was familiar with New York, having lived there as a child besides making fairly regular visits, and I liked the city. Chicago, it seemed to me, was more rigid and conservative—a rectangular city. New York was diagonal and free. I felt the need for injecting these qualities into my work.

This marked sensitivity to environment is a characteristic that remains with Oldenburg to this day. He still feels the need to change his environment at the dictate of his work. Recently, as an example, he moved to California and lived there for almost a year in order to absorb a regional atmosphere that he felt was called for in a particular project in which he was involved.

In New York, Oldenburg found an inexpensive apartment on the Lower East Side and a job at the Cooper Union Museum Library. For the next three years (1956–1959), he was alone, dividing his time among the library where he earned his keep; the city whose presence he absorbed; and his apartment, where he continued working on his art.

> I was something of a recluse at the time. I knew hardly anybody in New York, and weeks would sometimes go by without my seeing or speaking to anyone outside the Library. I remember being completely taken by the city. I spent hours wandering around or staring out of a window in the Library that overlooked The Bowery.

> The streets, in particular, fascinated me. They seemed to have an existence of their own where I discovered a whole world of objects that I had never known before. Ordinary packages became sculpture in my eye, and I saw street refuse as elaborate accidental compositions.

It was in this period that Oldenburg's artistic focus began to change. When he came to New York, he thought of himself as a more-or-less classical figure-painter. The impact of the city changed this outlook. His concern gradually shifted from composition and paint to volume and form, from the purely visual to the tactile, from painting to sculpture.

This shift led directly to Oldenburg's first one-man show. In May 1959—three years after he had come to New York and seven years after he had decided to make art his lifework—he exhibited a series of these newly realized sculptures at the Judson Gallery in Greenwich Village. The objects that Oldenburg created were inspired by the streets that held so much fascination for him. They consisted, for the most part, of abstract sculpture made of wood, paper, and string—materials commonly found on the street. Many of the pieces were based on the clumsy packages that Oldenburg had seen derelicts carrying about with them. These were made with paper wrapped about a frame or a real object and tied with string. In some cases, lines were painted on the paper in various tones of gray and black.

An additional feature of this first one-man show was a number of poems and verbal impressions that Oldenburg composed in his street wanderings. These short poems, blown up into large type, were exhibited on the gallery walls alongside the artist's sculpture.

Though the exhibit was neither a critical nor a financial success, the work from this period—which Oldenburg called "White Objects"—proved a crucial step in the development of the artist. In the creation of these objects, Oldenburg made a tentative start at a systematic style that has since become characteristic. Here, for the first time, he deliberately established an arbitrary set of rules or limitations within which he worked. His materials, for example, were limited to paper, wood, string, and other things that one might find in the street. Color was severely restricted to tones of white, gray, and black.

An arbitrary set of rules is not a new idea in art. Most art is created within clearly defined limits. In music, for example, there is the familiar sonata form, which provided the framework for the bulk of classical composition. In poetry, there are various metric devices in addition to such strict forms as the sonnet, rondo, and couplet. In painting, we have the example of the medieval religious artists, who created masterpieces within a severely prescribed framework. In my own experi-

63

ence, I find that this approach not only helps focus my energies, but also allows me to generate a tension in my work that would be lacking without this discipline.

Following "White Objects," Oldenburg embarked on a period of experiment that crystallized into two distinct, though related, themes: "The Ray Gun" and "The Street."

The Ray Gun spelled backward, "Nug Yar," or "New York" represented an exploration of the simple horizontal–vertical relationship whose most obvious manifestation is in the hand gun. As a symbol, the Ray Gun is phallic and universal. It is a theme that engenders endless variation and has appeared in all of Oldenburg's subsequent periods.

The Ray Gun is everywhere. It occurs in a sneaker turned upside down, in an ice-cream soda with a straw, in a free-form cocktail table, in a truck, and even the map of the United States can be considered an expression of this form. As utilized by Oldenburg, this theme provides a well of formal invention, a source on which the artist lavishes his highly developed sense of form, color, and wit.

This exploration of the horizontal–vertical relationship provided the basis for Oldenburg's second exhibit, also held at the Judson Gallery, from January to March 1960. The show was planned as an evocation of the street, and all phases of the construction of this environment were open to the public. Working with Jim Dine, who built a house for the environment, Oldenburg constructed his street on the basis of the Ray Gun concept of creating art out of the ordinary, common, nondescript aspects of our world.

Developing simultaneously with The Ray Gun, Oldenburg's Street period was shown two months later at the Reuben Gallery, in May 1960. The work from this phase consisted of cardboard-and-burlap sculptures and reliefs. The figure of a man and woman, both grotesquely elongated and flattened; strange, vaguely familiar objects which appeared to be transformed by the natural street erosion of cars and feet; cardboard sheets with city hieroglyphics scrawled on the surface—this was the world that Oldenburg had found in the street.

Although the work from this period had only limited exposure and was for the most part neglected, it brought Oldenburg's art to the attention of forward-looking galleries and collectors. In these odd sculptures and reliefs, the artist had discovered a new way of looking at the world. Here was a unique blend of the fantastic and the real that transformed the most ordinary objects into formal esthetic statements with undeniable visual power.

After the exhibit at the Reuben Gallery, Oldenburg felt the need to put this phase behind him. The city had exhausted him. He spent the summer in Provincetown, Massachusetts, in order to get away. Here, he turned his attention to the sea and the beach and created a number of weathered wood collages in the shape of flags. Some of these were shown in a group show entitled "New Forms, New Media," at the Martha Jackson Gallery early in the Fall of 1960. The artist had moved uptown.

> When I returned to New York after that summer on the Cape, I drove around the city one day with Jimmy Dine. By chance, we drove through Orchard Street, both sides of which are packed with small stores. As we drove, I remember having a vision of "The Store." I saw, in my mind's eye, a complete environment based on this theme. Again, it seemed to me that I had discovered a new world. I began wandering through stores—all kinds and all over—as though they were museums. I saw the objects displayed in windows and on counters as precious works of art.

This experience inspired Oldenburg's next phase. He began a systematic study of stores and store objects, absorbing the feel and color of that world. First, he made numerous drawings and copious notes on his impressions and ideas. These led, in turn, to the formation of a set of rules that determined the creative limits.

> The Street was a metaphor for line. The Store became a metaphor for color. In an East Side paint store, I found a line of paints, Frisco Enamel, which came in seven particularly bright colors that seemed to symbolize the store to me. These colors became my palette. The paint would be used straight from the can without any mixing or blending of color to paint reliefs of store objects. These would be made with burlap or muslin dipped in plaster and imposed over a modeled screen or chicken-wire frame.

Once the rules were established, Oldenburg proceeded to make the objects envisioned for his store. Works from this phase were first shown at the Martha Jackson Gallery in an exhibition entitled "Environments, Situations, and Spaces," organized by Rolf Nelson and Steven Joy in March 1961.

Oldenburg was, however, dissatisfied with the installation and decided to make a more complete exposition of the theme in his own studio, a Lower East Side storefront called the Ray Gun Manufacturing Company. He continued making additional pieces and opened his store in December 1961.

The exhibit was an immediate commercial and artistic success. In this store, Oldenburg created a total environment. The store and the objects combined to create a single esthetic statement under complete control of the artist. This period extended over some two years (1961–1962) and was divided into two distinct, but simultaneous phases. One was concerned with the manufactured object, and the other, with food.

After Oldenburg's first Store exhibit closed at the end of January 1962, the Ray Gun Manufacturing Company was changed to the Ray Gun Theater. Here, in the same Lower East Side storefront, Oldenburg presented a series of Happenings—an experimental theater wherein the artist extends his range to include sound, movement, and live people in his compositions.

That Spring, Oldenburg's Happenings became a New York fixture and people trekked down to the Ray Gun Theater on weekends to see *Store Days, Nekropolis, Injun, Voyages,* and *World's Fair.* Oldenburg designed and built the sets for each production and assigned the people involved specific movements, occasional speaking lines, and roles. In the construction of the sets, the artist made a number of large, bulky items out of burlap and canvas stuffed with paper or rags. He incorporated this technique into his formal art production as "soft sculpture."

A second version of "The Store" was shown at the Green Gallery in the Fall of 1962. Oldenburg worked in the gallery that Summer preparing the exhibit. He was always sensitive to his environment, and the objects that he created here differed subtly from those created and shown in the Lower East Side storefront. They were bigger, for one thing, and here the artist introduced his "soft sculpture"—objects made of cloth and plastic that could be manipulated.

> The Green Gallery offered a large expanse of open space. This, to an extent, dictated the size of the objects made for the exhibit. An equal influence was provided by the immediate surroundings of the gallery. Fifty-seventh Street is full of stores and showrooms that display large objects—cars, pianos, furniture, rugs. Seeing these things daily, as I did that Summer, compelled the creation of equally large objects.

A hamburger large enough to sleep on together with a pair of pants to fit a giant; bold reliefs painted with bright enamel; pies; a display of bras and underpants, caps and shoes, ladies' handbags—these represent the environment of "The Store." Individually, they are delightful works, full of humor and fantasy, and appear to be the spontaneous creations of an uninhibited child.

The appearance of spontaneity and freedom is, however, deceptive. They are the result of labor and discipline. They are the function of a highly developed eye which has learned to see beyond surface appearance. They represent deeply experienced truths about illusion and reality. Oldenburg has discovered spiritual meanings in material things. And these meanings are so strange and marvelous that he has had to create a new vocabulary in which to express them.

A hamburger, in the artist's experience, becomes a complex, multi-leveled symbol. One aspect can be interpreted as an expression of our time. The hamburger tells the story of fast cars, highways, and road-side stands. It is a food that is quickly prepared and even more quickly consumed. It is symbolic of a new, swift, mobile existence, of a unique national experience.

A more subtle interpretation reveals the hamburger as a manifestation of the oval—a perfect, universal form. The rounded, voluptuous bun has a distinctly feminine presence, its texture evocative of soft flesh. It is a passive, receptive form. Here, in one of the most popular and characteristic of American foods, we have an almost perfect female expression.

An ice-cream cone, on the other hand, is a distinctly masculine symbol that expresses another universal form—the cone. Here we have the ultimate phallic projection. The cone is a thrusting, dynamic shape, and in its manifestation as ice-cream cone it is rigid and rough. It is the inevitable complement to and alter side of the female hamburger.

In his search for significant images, Oldenburg has discovered fascinating relationships. He has made a study of forms as they occur in manufactured objects and has traced a unifying mystique that underlies what appears to be arbitrary choice.

A visitor to his studio once noticed an object that Oldenburg had made. It was a vaguely wedge-shaped piece of plaster crudely splattered with aluminum paint. He picked it up and tried to identify it. "It's a lady's handbag," he said as he turned the object about in his hand. "No, it's an iron. No, a typewriter. No, a toaster. No, it's a piece of pie." Oldenburg was delighted. The object, which was nothing more than a shape the artist had been toying with, was exactly what the visitor had described. All the objects he named were embodied in that small, wedge-shaped bit of painted plaster.

This equivalency of forms in different objects fascinates Oldenburg, and he utilizes this phenomenon in his work. He has developed an elaborate lexicon of equivalent objects: Ice-cream cone = sailboat; hamburger bun = cap; Mickey Mouse = armchair; a wedge of pie = knife; handbag = typewriter. These multifaceted objects trace a subconscious relationship that underlies even the most casual choice of form in the manufacture of objects.

With the completion of the second Store exhibit, Oldenburg felt that he had exhausted, for the time being, both this phase of his work and New York City. Feeling the need for change, he and his wife moved to California where they set up housekeeping in a bungalow in Venice. The change was dictated, in part, by a new project that Oldenburg became involved with.

Both the Street and the Store periods were inspired by New York, which seems to embody these two aspects of our reality. When I became interested in the home as a thematic source, I felt the need to move. California, it seemed to me, was much more home-oriented. In New York, for example, we lived in a walk-up apartment. In California, we lived in a house complete with a little patch of garden. It seemed the ideal place in which to work on this new phase.

The Home was, of course, to be an entirely different entity from either The Store or The Street. The Street represented a metaphor for line; The Store, for color. The Home, on the other hand, would be a metaphor for volume. Again, there was a new set of rules. In The Home, there could be no painting or brushwork. Everything had to be manufactured. Colors would be used as they appear in natural and manufactured objects. And all the objects would be related to the home.

The first work from this new period was a Bedroom that was shown in a group exhibit of environments at the Sidney Janis Gallery in the Winter of 1963. A brilliantly conceived and executed work, The Bedroom consisted of a bed, dresser, chair, and accessories done in exaggerated "Modern."

> The layout of the room, along with the individual pieces, were determined by the dimensions of a particular room at the Janis Gallery. I measured the room carefully before I left for California and had the feel and atmosphere of that space in mind while I worked. One of my principal problems in preparing an exhibit is the fact that gallery space does not change. It remains constant. My work, on the other hand, is always in flux, and often the idea and the available space do not coincide.

A more extensive exploration of the Home theme was revealed in Oldenburg's first one-man show at the Janis Gallery in the Spring of 1964. In many respects, The Home is a natural extension of The Store. Though the imagery and objects are sometimes similar in appearance, they differ profoundly in essence. A Home shirt, for example, has an entirely different presence from a Store shirt. One is on display, an enticement to buy; the other is functional, an indispensable part of the everyday life that centers in The Home.

After the close of this exhibit, Oldenburg and his wife went to Europe, where they stayed for six months. They visited the Venice Biennale, where his works were on display, and toured the Continent. It was hardly a vacation, however, for during this sojourn Oldenburg prepared a complete exhibit that was shown at the Sonnabend Gallery in Paris and designed sets in Italy for an Antonioni movie that may or may not be completed.

Claes Oldenburg is a big man who projects an impression of strength and immense reserves of energy. Thinning blond hair, blue eyes, often hiding behind a detached, deadpan expression, there is nothing obvious in either his manner or physical appearance to suggest the artist. He could be the superintendent of a Bay Ridge apartment house; one of those nameless, shirt-sleeved men who sit in the bleachers at Shea Stadium watching the Mets, a hot dog in one hand and a can of beer in the other; or he might be a Wall Street broker. Yet, appearances are deceptive. Claes Oldenburg has subordinated his entire being to the pursuit of an original, intensely personal vision. His artistic goals are ambitious, and he applies himself to their realization with complete dedication.

If the modern man is typically other-directed, then Oldenburg must be considered an atavist, a throw-back to an older, now rare personality type. He is the completely inner-directed man. His personality is built on a framework of values and goals that are unaffected by the currents of the world. He goes his own way.

Some years ago, he recorded his artistic credo for the catalogue of a group exhibit in which he was involved. That commitment remains the same:

> I am for an art that takes its form from the lines of life, that twists and extends impossibly and accumulates and spits and drips and is as sweet and stupid as life itself.

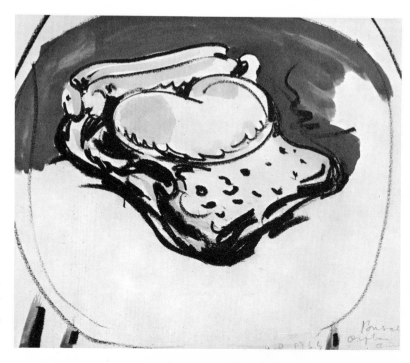

Drawing, Claes Oldenburg.
Courtesy Sidney Janis Gallery, New York. Photograph: Geoffrey Clements.

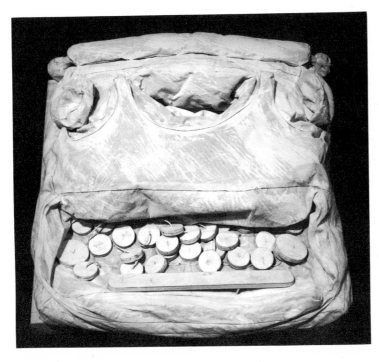

"Ghost Typewriter,"
Claes Oldenburg.
*Courtesy Sidney Janis
Gallery, New York.
Photograph:
Geoffrey Clements.*

"Toaster,"
Claes Oldenburg.
*Photographed in
Sidney Janis Gallery,
New York.*

"Ghost Toaster,"
Claes Oldenburg.
*Courtesy Sidney Janis
Gallery, New York.
Photograph:
Geoffrey Clements.*

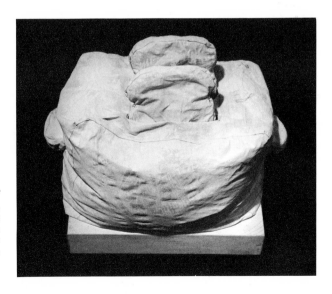

Can corset bar
be broken down
into parts-
to sell

in
Case

show slides
at topy.

metal
strips,

Sam — 3d
prints?

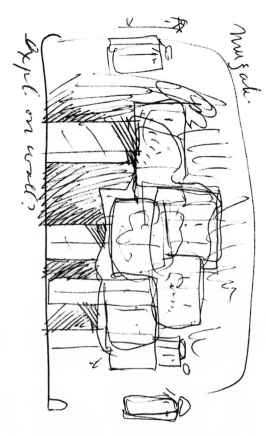

growing
apple.   BOXES=
room

THE ∞ HOME

Details from Claes Oldenburg's notebook

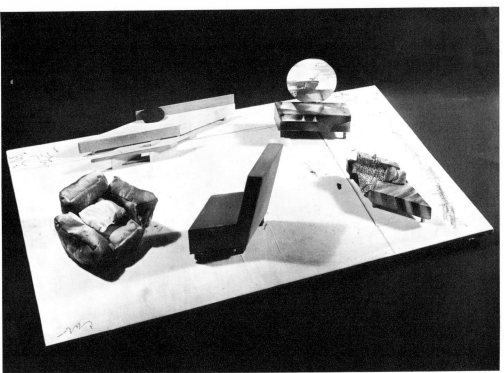

"Miniature Scale Models: Dresser, Three Chairs, Sofa, and Cocktail Table," Claes Oldenburg.
Courtesy Sidney Janis Gallery, New York. Photograph: Geoffrey Clements.

Pat and Claes Oldenburg

JAMES ROSENQUIST

While attending the University of Minnesota, I worked one summer for an industrial decorating company. At least, that's what they called themselves. Actually, we traveled through the Midwest painting the outsides of warehouses and huge storage bins. Some of them were ten stories high and half a city block long. We painted everything the same color. I remember miles of the same monotonous shade of gray.

One day, we began working on a group of these storage bins—I think that they held surplus wheat—and this fellow began painting one of them by himself. Now picture this scene: there's this stretch of wall at least as big as a football field, and way down in one corner is this little man with a bucket of paint—gray paint—and an eight-inch brush in his hand. Slowly, deliberately, hopelessly, he begins to apply paint to that endless, unrelieved expanse of wall.

Who should come walking by but the foreman. The guy painting did not notice him and kept right on painting in the same slow, lackadaisical way. The foreman must have stood there watching him for a good ten minutes; I guess he was building up a head of steam. When he couldn't take any more, the foreman hollered: "WHAT THE HELL DO YOU THINK YOU'RE DOING?" Believe me, that foreman knew how to yell.

The guy painting, though, just turned around, paintbrush in hand. He stared at the foreman and then glanced back over his shoulder at the huge wall. "Hunh?" he said. On the road, a trailer truck roared by and an airplane flew overhead.

The story describes a bizarre and rather wonderful visual experience; it describes the world of James Rosenquist. There is a juxtaposition of visual elements here that is at once ordinary and utterly extraordinary. It is a juxtaposition that could have occurred only at this particular point in time. Here is all the extravagance of imagery—the disjointed elements and the forced perspective that have come to be the identifying characteristics of the art of James Rosenquist.

Rosenquist tells the story with relish, emphasizing points with bodily gestures and pantomiming the various incidents. As he tells the story, however, one becomes aware that words are not his preferred medium. He projects his impressions most strongly through gesture and expression. One gets the feeling that he would be more comfortable expressing himself pictorially.

The story also reveals the unique visual sensitivity at the core of Rosenquist's artistic statement. His work is characterized by the same bizarre, seemingly disconnected imagery. Here is the frozen moment that explores multiple levels of reality as they are revealed in a fleeting passage of time. Here is the same strange and wonderful juxtaposition of elements that is so much a part of the visual phenomena of our time.

Rosenquist's response to this reality is poetic, almost mystical. His vision is a function of this individual reaction. The reaction, in turn, is the result of the million and one influences that went into the creation of James Rosenquist the man. Rosenquist's ability to project this inner vision onto his canvases is a function of skill and technique. The skill is, in turn, a result of the years of study and application that went into the development of James Rosenquist the artist.

He was born in Grand Forks, North Dakota. His father was an airplane mechanic, and the family moved a good deal within the same general region—the Dakotas and Minnesota. He grew up under the huge expanses of the Great Prairie. In its startling landscape, there was more than enough stimulation to rouse a natural visual sensitivity. As a boy, Rosenquist enjoyed sketching, drawing, and just looking at the world around him.

When he enrolled at the University of Minnesota, Rosenquist had no clearly defined ambitions. His interest in art was vague and formless. It needed an outside impetus to come to fruition. This impetus was provided by Cameron Booth, an art teacher at the university. Rosenquist met Booth when he took his course during his first year at the university. Booth proved to be a sympathetic and influential teacher. He recognized Rosenquist's native ability and encouraged his efforts. The young artist studied with Booth for the next three years.

It was during this third year that Booth suggested that Rosenquist try for a competitive scholarship award to the Art Students League in

New York. This application proved to be a turning-point in the young artist's life. He won the scholarship and came to New York in the Fall of 1955.

> When I first came to New York, I lived for a while in a small furnished room on West 59th Street. Directly across the street, the New York Coliseum area was under demolition. I remember once sitting on my front stoop eating a sandwich. The demolition across the street was going on at a furious pace, and the air was full of dust. As I sat there, I watched the sandwich in my hand change from white to dull gray as the dust settled.

After graduating from the Art Students League, Rosenquist continued painting and working on his own. He supported himself during this period with a variety of jobs. At times he worked as a chauffeur, a butler, and a billboard painter. Although he lived in New York, he made occasional trips back to Minnesota and North Dakota.

On one of these trips, Rosenquist helped with the spring plowing on his uncle's farm—five hundred acres of good farm land in western Minnesota.

> We got up early in the morning—about 5 o'clock, which I wasn't used to—and ate a huge breakfast. Four cups of coffee, waffles, and about three big scoops of ice cream. My uncle, who was something of an alcoholic, supplemented his breakfast with whiskey. Then we went out—it was still dark—oiled up the plows, gassed up the tractors, and got the rigs ready. This took about two or three hours, so we went back into the house for another breakfast.
>
> By now, it was about 8 o'clock in the morning, and the work with the plows really put an edge on our appetites. Ham, three or four eggs, stacks of buttered toast, and steaming hot cups of coffee—plus more whiskey for my uncle—and we were ready to go back to work. We went out onto the fields with the three plows and ripped furrows, bouncing and bucking across the land until noon. We stopped for lunch back at the house, and this time we really ate.
>
> After lunch, we gassed up the tractors, checked the rigs, and the three plows went out again. We didn't get back till 6 that night. I figured that this was just about the longest day I had ever known. I was tired. But, after another huge meal, we went out and started to plow some more.

That night the moon came up just as the sun went down, and, for a few minutes, the furrows were lit up from both sides—by the sinking sun on one side and the rising moon on the other. The noise from the tractors was deafening, and they rattled and bounced across that field, but it was a beautiful sight. Later that night, the stars came out. Then a storm came up, and huge clouds piled up in the sky to hide the stars, but it blew over fast and the stars came out again.

'Long about midnight, one of the other drivers ambled over to me. He was black with dust, but there were white circles around his eyes outlining the goggles he wore while plowing. I remember that he reminded me of a bear. He came over, looked up at the sky, and said, "It looks like a clear day tomorrow."

I could never understand before how people stood the terrible monotony of farm life, of working the land. But, after that night, I think I learned why people do it and why they love the life.

After these brief interludes, however, Rosenquist always returned to New York, where he continued painting. He managed to maintain a loft while working at various jobs and painted whenever he had a free moment. During this period, Rosenquist experimented with various styles and media which were mostly in the abstract-expressionist vein.

As an artist, Rosenquist was something of a loner. He never was a part of any particular circle and worked, for the most part, by himself. Occasionally he would make a tour of the New York museums and galleries, but these were rare events. He preferred to rely on himself, to develop a style that was independent of the things being done around him. In this way, Rosenquist worked steadily, perfecting the skills and techniques of the painter. He felt the need, however, to devote more of his time to his art. He needed long stretches of undisturbed time to think and work.

By the early part of 1960, I had managed to save enough money from my regular jobs to live on for a year if I managed carefully. This year would be devoted completely to painting. I got a loft down in Coenties Slip, below the financial district, and, for the first time since I got out of school, I was able to spend whole days and weeks in the loft. Most of the time I would paint, but there were also long stretches when I just sat there and thought without any interruptions. Sometimes I sat there from 9 in the morning until 4 in the afternoon watching other people go to and from their jobs. I never felt that I was wasting time. It felt great to be free of a routine job.

Then, suddenly, it seemed as though ideas came floating in to me through the window. All I had to do was snatch them out of the air and begin painting. Everything seemed to fall into place—the idea, the composition, the imagery, the colors, everything began to work.

Within a few months, Rosenquist developed the style and imagery that have become so characteristic of his work. He recognized the power and validity of the style and felt that he had discovered the idiom that could express his most deeply felt reactions to the world around him. Whether the world would agree with his judgment remained to be seen.

This question was, however, to be answered sooner than Rosenquist ever dared hope. Although he did not know it at the time, Rosenquist's paintings were closely related to those of the other artists who were to be identified with the pop movement. Working alone and completely independently of the others, Rosenquist had developed a style out of his most personal experiences. His imagery derived from the ordinary and commonplace visual associations of the American landscape.

This concern with common images, occurring as it did among this group of artists, reflected a profound change in esthetic values. Rosenquist, along with the other artists in the group, was sensitive to this change, and his style represents an individual response to this new atmosphere. Like the others, Rosenquist stumbled on his imagery. His first paintings in the style were no more than experiments. He realized, however, that this particular imagery and style were right. It expressed something valid and important in the esthetic reality of the time.

His work came to the attention of Richard Bellamy, of the Green Gallery, who arranged Rosenquist's first one-man show, in February 1962. That exhibit was an immediate success. It reinforced the growing awareness that a new artistic movement had developed. Rosenquist's bizarre imagery and poetic vision struck a responsive chord in some of the most influential collectors—if not among the majority of established critics. His work was glossed over at first as nothing more than an interesting maverick development. Indeed, he was described by one critic as a "billboard painter gone legit."

Although there is an element of truth in this statement, it misses the point. Rosenquist had worked as a billboard painter, and the influence of this experience on his art cannot be denied. But he worked on a farm and as a chauffeur, and these experiences exerted an influence on his work. What was omitted in this critique is the fact that Rosenquist was an artist with years of experience and thorough training. As an artist, he knew what he was doing. The extravagant imagery utilized in his paintings was neither accidental nor arbitrary. It has the same relationship to his work as the cubist idiom, for example, has to the work of Picasso. This was a vocabulary used by the artist to project a specific esthetic impression. The fact that the vocabulary was used skillfully and with verve was overlooked.

His approach to painting is physical and completely sensual. Once he has developed an idea to the point of visualization, Rosenquist works quickly, furiously, throwing himself bodily into the task of creation. First the rough outlines of the subjects are chalked in, and then paint is applied in an explosion of activity.

The feverish pace of his work is reflected in his loft. It is a shambles. The walls are covered with pages cut from magazines and rough sketches. The floor is strewn with discarded cans, brushes, left-over materials, pieces of canvas, tools, and other debris. As he works, Rosenquist moves through this chaos as though in a dream. All his energies are focused on the painting, and he remains oblivious to his surroundings.

> Every now and then, it gets so bad that even I have to clean it up. But then I do another painting or two and it looks exactly the same as before.

Rosenquist's ideas are arrived at by a rather circuitous route. An incident or a particular scene may provide the germinal motif, or it may derive from a thought or a passing fancy. One of his most recent paintings, for example, is a stark depiction of a large mixing bowl, seen from the top; filled with whipped cream that is being scooped out of the bowl with a spatula. The genesis of this painting is typical.

At one time, I shared a loft with another painter. He would paint all day long. Then at night he would study his work, shake his head in disgust, and proceed to scrape the paint down from the canvas. This went on for days. He would paint all day and then scrape everything down at night. This process seemed to make the artist an unnecessary middleman. Why not just pour the paint on the floor and leave the canvas clean?

One day, while thumbing through a magazine, I saw a picture of a bowl of whipped cream. The image of the whipped cream being scraped out of the bowl gave me the idea of doing a painting of that painter scraping an illusionistic rendering of depth onto the floor.

Occasionally, an idea presents problems that challenge the ingenuity of the artist. The creation of Rosenquist's free-standing sculpture entitled "Capillary Action II" provides a good example of this experience.

A few years ago, I saw a photograph of a meadow with a tree standing in the middle. I couldn't get that image out of my mind, where it kept flashing on and off—extremely artificial in one phase and then completely natural again. This experience made me aware of a startling aspect of our present landscape in which nature becomes increasingly modified by man until the natural and artificial blend into each other. This awareness prompted the creation of an art work that could somehow project these two opposite feelings—naturalness and artificiality. My first reaction was to paint a landscape as realistically as I could make it while retaining the artificiality that one sees, for example, in the Museum of Natural History exhibits. After thinking about the problem, however, I decided that I could achieve my ends best by using an actual tree—a small sapling, perhaps—in a free-standing sculpture. I had a very definite idea as to how that tree should look. I wanted to saw a slot down the middle of the tree and insert a canvas with an electric neon rectangle into the slot. Finding the tree that would agree with my notion of what a tree should look like proved to be extremely difficult. Ray Donarski, a close friend, and I spent a whole day and part of a night driving all over Westchester and New Jersey looking for this tree. We couldn't find it and had to settle for a reasonable facsimile.

This experience became a bizarre exercise in asserting oneself as an artist. The artist has control over the nature of things he puts into his canvas, and I wanted to assert this right yet not destroy nature in the process. I had an idea of a tree, but nature refused to supply that tree. I had to compromise. By sacrificing a real tree in the creation of this electrified tree image, I hoped to express the problem of the artist's use of nature while opposing its destruction. I am still very much involved with this problem of nature, man, and artist. Right now, I am working on a series of plastic-wave sculpture-paintings involved with the sea that refer to this same problem.

Rosenquist has achieved an enviable professional level. His paintings are in demand, and his reputation has become firmly established. He has had highly successful one-man shows in America and in Europe and has seen his work exhibited in most of the major modern-art museums of the world.

The process of painting, of realizing the inner vision, however, remains the same. For Rosenquist, this task remains a formidable challenge.

A reality may turn me on, and I hope that my finished picture will do the same or better, but the process in between is still nerve-racking.

Photograph: United Press International

"Vestigial Appendage,"
James Rosenquist.
Collection Giuseppe Panza, Milan.
Photograph: Eric Pollitzer.

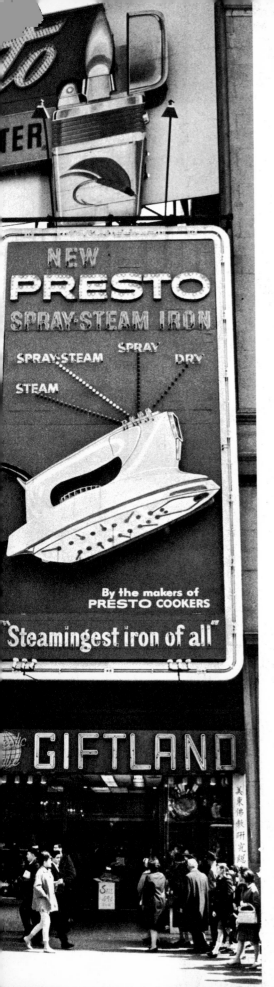

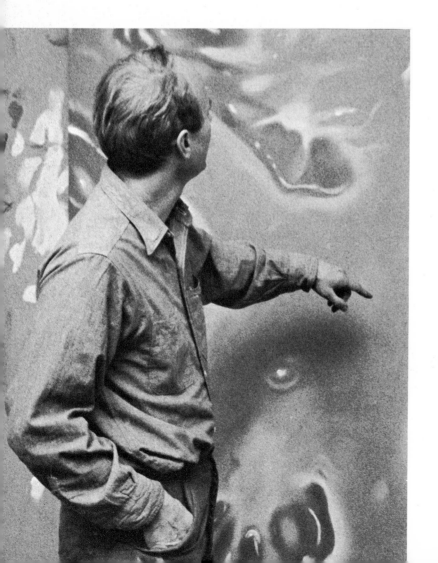

Andy Warhol

There is a small portrait of the late Marilyn Monroe by Andy Warhol that is typical of his best work. The subject is in no way extraordinary, but the execution represents a departure from accepted standards. The technique, a mechanically reproduced image daubed with garish colors, is outrageous. The background color is grape; and the too-familiar face, silk-screened onto the canvas, is highlighted with yellow over the hair, pink on the skin, blue over the eyes with chartreuse eye shadows, and a splash of red over half-opened lips that is repeated in a patch of dress that shows at the neck.

At first glance, the subject appears banal, the treatment vulgar, as though the artist sought the lowest common denominator in the visual resources at his command. The brazen colors scream for attention. The painting could serve as an image on a poster advertising a girlie show.

Once the shock of subject-recognition and technique is overcome, however, the portrait can be appreciated on many levels. Considered for its painterly qualities alone, for example, a great deal of merit is revealed. There is authority in the composition, control in the artless manner in which the image is projected onto the canvas, vitality in the arrogant use of color, and, most important, a high order of sensitivity in the selection of image to be reproduced.

These qualities, though strong enough to allow the work to stand on its own without reference to subject matter, represent the surface of the painting. They are the means by which the artist achieves his ends. It is in the interplay between painting and observer that the depths of the portrait are exposed.

On one level, the painting can be considered an abstraction of that ubiquitous woman whose idealized features assail our eyes from almost anywhere we chance to look. She stares down on us from billboards and posters; we see her in magazines and newspapers, confront her on movie and television screens. We may or may not like her, but it is impossible to escape her presence. She is of our world, as much a part of the landscape as a tree or a cloud or the empty beer cans that drift along our highways, the result of a bizarre snowfall. On this level, the painting serves as an expression of our time, a focus on an important facet of our world. No one can deny the veracity of the image or fail to perceive the truth that is revealed in the work—and truth, the poet tells us, is beauty.

On another level, we can consider the subject of the portrait. Here is Marilyn Monroe garbed in the mask of the goddess. As goddess, she is bigger than life. She is a star who exists on Olympian heights. Yet behind the mask is a woman, and the woman was vulnerable. She was made of flesh and half-realized dreams—hardly the stuff that gods are made of.

The portrait of Marilyn Monroe tells the story of a human being transformed, of a woman changed into a commercial property. She has been carefully manufactured, packaged, and sold like a can of soup. Her painted mask is reproduced endlessly until it is no longer possible to say where the mask ends and the woman begins. Illusion and reality become confused. The tragic transformation is complete. A novelist might tell her story in a hundred-thousand words; a playwright, in three hours behind the proscenium arch. Andy Warhol has told it in a small painting, a silk-screened image daubed with garish colors.

On all levels, the work grips the emotions. It communicates, becoming something more than a skillful organization of line and color. The subject of the painting lives on the canvas. How this magic is accomplished is a high mystery. Who can say what sparks a combination of color and form, causing a composition to ignite in the eye of the beholder? Who knows why certain images are capable of moving a viewer deeply while the same images, slightly altered, remain lifeless? These qualities are the result of a dark alchemy that can never be fully explained. They represent the subtle boundary between art and craft.

The painting that appears so obvious at first glance proves to be a complex creation. It is blatant and subtle, naïve and sophisticated, gaudy and beautiful. It is both meaningful and meaningless; it exists on many levels of interpretation. It is much like the man who created it.

Andy Warhol is a complex man who defies classification. Like the portrait of Marilyn Monroe, he, too, wears a mask—a contrived image that serves as a buffer between him and the world. He, too, is a web of contradictions without obvious resolution.

In casual relations with people, Warhol is gentle, considerate, and bland. His conversation is irrelevant, skirting all meaningful issues. Though he is interested in people and is sensitive to their individuality, he is wary and gives little of himself. He never loses either his temper or his composure. He has come to terms with the world.

Physically, Andy Warhol is in no way unusual. He can be thought of as an Everyman. He is medium: medium height, medium weight, medium coloring, medium age. Seen from a distance, he merges into the background. You would not notice him in the street. In a crowd, he becomes a nameless face, as unobtrusive as smoke.

In more intimate contact, however, the artfully contrived mask projects a unique personality. The image that he presents to the world is as carefully composed as any of his paintings. From the clothes he wears to the manner in which he combs his hair; from the diffident, naïve speech patterns to the fluid, oddly graceful walk—everything about the man is calculated to enhance the image. And the creation works. Like a fully realized painting or sculpture, Andy Warhol has a presence. His image deflects space, drawing the eye and the emotions along lines determined by the artist.

Seen up close, the mask is striking. The hair, brown and artificially streaked with gray, is worn casually as though no comb ever gave it shape. The skin is pallid, almost white, with a texture never coarsened by exposure to sun or wind. The eyes are soft, expressive. They are the eyes of a fragile night creature who discovers himself living in the blaze of an alien, but fascinating, world. The lips are petulant and sensuous, and the entire visage is suffused with sensitivity. It could be the mask of a saint—or a satyr.

The mask serves a dual purpose. It attracts and obscures. It satisfies an exhibitionist tendency while it hides the man. It is theatrical, obvious, shocking, and completely disarming. It focuses all attention on the surface. Behind the mask, the man remains inviolate. Andy Warhol has erected an armor that turns aside every probe before it can reach too deep—a shield that guards a raw edge of sensitivity.

During an interview, a reporter once asked Warhol about his background. Warhol's answer was typically enigmatic: "Why don't you make it up?" he suggested.

His answer is, of course, part of the pose. The probe is deflected. Yet, it is not just a simple evasion. Warhol tells us, in effect, that a human being is a complex creature that is something more than the mere sum of his days. Warhol prefers to be without a background and asks us to leave it at that. Very well. He is like Athena, who sprang fully armed and ready for battle from the head of Zeus or like the hero of a grade-B western who emerges from a shadowy past to accomplish high deeds in Arizona and then recedes into an equally shadowy future. He is the second, apostate Adam who sees the world through new eyes, compelled to test and question everything.

Yet the carefully constructed armor does crumble. The man, so difficult to know, is revealed in his work. One aspect can be seen in the delight he feels for his environment. He enjoys our world and accepts it as it is, discovering esthetic values in the most prosaic elements. A can of soup, seen through his eyes, becomes a universal symbol, and a cardboard carton becomes the subject for artistic investigation. This ability to see beneath the surface makes even the simple act of walking down the street an esthetic experience. Warhol notices everything—a billboard, a prowling cat, the texture of a wall, a man unknowingly striking an attitude of face or body that reveals unplumbed depths of his being—and everything is utilized in his work.

This quality is reflected in Warhol's paintings of everyday objects. Campbell Soup cans, Coca-Cola bottles, money, cardboard cartons, matchbooks, shipping labels—all have been transformed by the artist into esthetic statements. He has infused these homely objects with his own sense of delight, and this delight has heightened their reality, elevating them into the realm of art.

In the process, Warhol has challenged the unwritten code that establishes a hierarchy of suitable artistic subjects. He questions the logic that makes it permissible to paint an apple, but not a salami or a Campbell Soup can. Warhol refuses to recognize any arbitrary limit to the subject matter of his work.

The celebration of the banal represents, however, only one aspect of these paintings. All Warhol's work is multileveled and can be interpreted in many ways. Though these works express his delight with everyday objects, they go beyond a simple presentation of everyday things. They also express Warhol's attitude to the problems of the artist in attempting to express the realities of the twentieth-century world.

This attitude was made explicit during a television interview, when a reporter and camera crew visited Warhol in his loft. The artist was working on his carton sculpture. About a hundred wooden boxes, all painted the same cardboard-brown color, were lined up along the floor. Warhol and an assistant moved from one box to the next, silk-screening an identical image on each box—the printing from a Campbell Soup carton in this case. Sometimes Andy would print the design, sometimes his assistant. It was a smooth, well-coordinated activity—a production line in a surrealist sweat shop.

In the course of the interview, Warhol was asked why he used a mechanical device to reproduce the design. "I tried doing them by hand," Andy told the television audience, "but I find it easier to use a screen. This way, I don't have to work on my objects at all. One of my assistants or anyone else, for that matter, can reproduce the design as well as I could."

Warhol's answer was consistent. Although it was true, it revealed nothing beyond the obvious fact that it is easier to reproduce an image mechanically than by hand. The question of why an artist should choose what appears to be such an easy way out remained unanswered.

The answer to this question provides another insight into the personality of Andy Warhol. Through this flaw in the armor, we glimpse a sensitivity acutely attuned to the environment, an intelligence that can pick out of the anarchic swirl of images and events one of the most salient characteristics of our time.

Duplication and repetition are new factors in the world. They occur neither in nature nor in handcrafts. They are a function of the machine, and the machine is the dominant influence of the twentieth century. For the first time since man appeared on earth, we are confronted with identical objects. We are inundated with them. Cars, clothes, cartons, cans, bottles, breads, pictures, homes, appliances, one exactly the same as another, engulf the world. Forty million people across the country can sit in darkened rooms and stare at an identical image on their television screens.

How does the artist, with his highly developed sensitivity, express these phenomena? Andy Warhol has done it by utilizing mechanical techniques, by using the machine to express the machine. What an audacious solution! What depths of the man are revealed in the gesture! This was not an easy way out. This was an innovation conceived by a bold, original imagination. This was a leap into a new world where old values and standards become meaningless.

But there is more in these banal cartons than has yet met the eye. Most of the cartons—indeed, most of Warhol's everyday objects—have to do with food. Food is, of course, a basic necessity. The manner in which it is obtained and distributed is elemental to all societies. It is a determining factor in mythology, architecture, social relations, religion, art—everything in a society.

The agricultural experience has changed little through the centuries—until now. The machine has intruded, irrevocably altering the age-old relation of man to the earth. Today, we depend on great factory farms for our food, and even the dairy herd is regulated by calculating machines that determine optimum schedules, feed, and milking procedures—also accomplished by machine—for maximum production.

What is true of food is true of all the other manufactured products we use in our daily lives. We can have all of our material needs satisfied by products *untouched by human hands*. Here is another new factor in the world. It represents a revolution that has been neither understood nor assimilated. In the advanced industrial countries of the world, we are just beginning to realize the scope of this change.

The machine is changing the face of the world, altering its colors, forms, and textures, as well as the familiar social orders of the past. The artist, above all others, must be sensitive to these shifts. It is his task to determine

> . . . What rough beast, its hour come at last
> slouches towards Bethlehem to be born?

Andy Warhol has accepted this challenge. In his elemental soup cans and cartons, in his awesome series of repeated-image paintings, he has given us an art for the twentieth century. He has created a new esthetic; a cold, mechanical, personality-purged expression; art untouched by human hands. The artist has become a machine.

It is a bold attempt that stakes out new vistas for the artist, obliterating the line that separates art and life. Warhol has taken a searching look at the world around him and has demonstrated the honesty and courage necessary to follow an idea to its conclusion. In so doing, he has created a new art that is measured against and is identical with the dimensions of the twentieth-century world. The machine has changed the world, and art, if it is to have any validity, must reflect this change.

The attempt also reveals a great deal about the man. It takes a special kind of person to venture into an entirely new dimension. Most of us—and this includes artists—are content to remain within the boundaries dictated by habit and custom, where familiar values and standards have been established to guide us. Andy Warhol must be included in that rare company who recognize no boundaries, who create their own standards and values.

Still another aspect of the man is revealed in the powerfully evocative "death-image" paintings. In this series, Warhol has used news photos of accidents, suicides, murders, riots, and other horrendous human activities; blown them up as large as life in some cases; and projected them onto huge canvases. The resulting works are strange, frightening creations that overwhelm the viewer with their realistic power.

These works reveal a creativity that exists close to the unconscious. In his search for artistic truths, Warhol has stripped away the layers of pretense and repression that obscure dark memories and knowledge all of us share. His imagery grips the imagination, striking a hauntingly responsive chord.

One painting, in particular, comes to mind. It is made from a photograph of the electric chair at Sing Sing prison. The murderous device stands in the middle of an empty room. In the upper right-hand corner of the room, we see a sign with the single word, "SILENCE," imprinted in bold letters.

Silence? This kind of mindless juxtaposition generates its own peculiar horror. Andy Warhol searches for these chance happenings and uses them to heighten the effect of his creations. They are akin to the found objects artists use in collage and assemblage.

These "death-image" paintings, which are among Warhol's toughest, reveal an unsuspected dimension of the man. They are, of course, paintings—visual devices designed to involve the viewer on an emotional as well as on a sensual level. The subject matter can be thought of as nothing more than a particularly evocative imagery. Yet the imagination that conceived them is tinged with more than a touch of morbidity. We catch a glimpse of a man flirting, half in love, with the idea of death. The morbid quality extends beyond the "death-image" series. It colors everything Warhol does. There is a hint of it in the repeated-image paintings of people, in the banks of stacked soup cans and Coca-Cola bottles, and even in his cartons.

In a way, all art is tinged with morbidity, with a fascination for death. Art is an attempt to immortalize a moment, to snatch a vision from the tyranny of time. Art rejects death and in the rejection embraces it. This double-edged sword cuts through all of Warhol's work, brushing everything with its aura.

We have penetrated the mask to catch a glimpse of a complex personality, but it is no more than a glimpse. A shy exhibitionist, a timidly bold innovator, a gently ruthless artist, a blend of contrasts and contradictions, an excess of sensitivity, Andy Warhol the man eludes us. He resists classification. He hides, avoiding irritating contacts with the world.

His mask is also the emblem of the oracle. It is the python mask donned by the priestess when, drunk with visionary excess, she proclaims the future in rough hexameters. Behind his mask, Andy Warhol, also drunk with visionary ardor, proclaims new beauties in reiterated mechanical images.

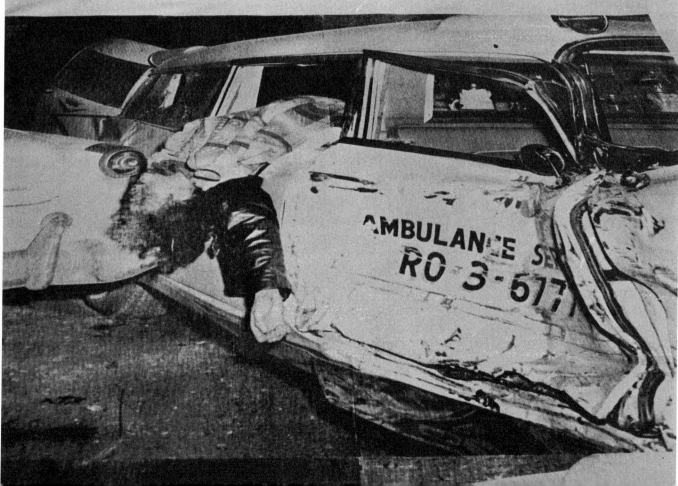

TOM WESSELMANN

Seated before a large, rectangular plywood board, he does nothing. He sits and stares, engrossed in a problem that dominates him completely. Arranged haphazardly on the board are a fan, an electric clock, a fluorescent lighting fixture, and an aluminum window screen. Occasionally he moves one or another of these elements and then stares again.

The objects on the board are related. All are common household articles found in every home. They are real. Beyond the purely functional aspect of each object is its shape, size, color, and psychological overtones. These are the primary concern of the artist. The fan, light fixture, and clock are round and about the same size; the window screen is rectangular and much larger. All are made of shiny, colorless metal —chrome, stainless steel, or polished aluminum. Their surfaces, though similar, differ subtly in texture and albedo.

The compositional problem posed to the artist is abstract—an esthetically satisfying arrangement of these common objects within the space limits of the board. It is complicated, however, by the functional aspect of each object. This factor must also be resolved within the given space. We begin to understand the scope of the task and the reason for the engrossment of the artist.

For Tom Wesselmann, the successful creation of a painting or collage represents the solution to a specific problem—in this case, an arrangement of the elements within the arbitrary space limit that will be characteristic of the function of each object while remaining compositionally sound and esthetically pleasing.

> When I begin working on a piece, I can never predict how long it will take me to finish. The way I work tends to be inconsistent because it is largely determined by the kind of piece I'm working on. A huge piece with billboard elements requires a great deal of manipulation, while a smaller piece jammed with appliances is readily set, to a certain extent, so that the piece is one-third solved almost at the very beginning. Most of my time is spent looking—either wondering what

in hell I'm going to do with that damn thing or in trying to become sensitive to it. With me, painting is generally a series of acceptances to which subsequent developments must conform. It is a process of narrowing the range of choice until there are no more choices. The process is largely sensual, a question of feelings and sensation; quite often, a physical catch in my stomach indicates the correct choice. I arrange and rearrange until the elements lock into place. When this happens, the composition develops a physical resistance to any further manipulation. Sometimes I have to then spend a day or two looking at it, trying to convince myself that it is really finished and right.

This feeling of compositional solidity is an important characteristic of Wesselmann's work. In his best efforts, the composition of the elements appears to be inevitable, as though there could be no other arrangement possible within that particular framework. Space is filled absolutely, and the composition is so precisely balanced that any change would destroy the equilibrium. Compositional solidity of this order is not easily achieved. Hours, sometimes days, are spent staring at his work. Delicate, miniscule adjustments are made and then abandoned. Many sketches and drawings are executed and studied as the composition is slowly molded into congruence with the inner vision.

Wesselmann's approach to art is classical, almost scholarly. He is involved with those problems of space and composition that have been the concern of the artist since art began. Each generation of artists, however, must confront these problems anew, must discover its own solutions within the context of its own world. Solutions that were valid twenty or even ten years ago are no longer applicable today. They can be used as a point of departure, their lessons applied to the work at hand, but they cannot be copied. To repeat the work of the past is to deny the truth of the present; and without truth there can be no beauty, no art.

There have been several influences on my work. The subject matter of my earliest portrait collages came directly from Hans Memling, the fifteenth-century Flemish painter, but the idea content was more influenced by such painters as Pollock and DeKooning. DeKooning's way of jamming his space to the bursting point and working hard against the edges of his canvas was especially influential. I also learned a lot from Matisse. I remember spending hours studying reproductions of his paintings. I would challenge him in imaginary conversations to tell me why he did each thing the way he did. "Why did you make that hand so big?" He would say, "See how that hand brings that part of the painting forward and frees the adjacent area so that it can move forward with it and laterally, independent of it." Often, in going over the same painting at another time, I would get different answers.

Wesselmann acknowledges his debt to the past, but does not use this heritage eclectically. He has applied the lessons of the past to his own expression. His originality manifests itself in two important areas. One of these is, of course, in his choice of subject matter.

Though he is not the first artist to utilize common images in his work, his use of them is unique. Among the objects Wesselmann incorporates into his collages are the vulgar and banal, as well as such "cultural" elements as reproductions of established masters. This is a conscious choice. He has transformed these very qualities of vulgarity and banality into a kind of musical key, or signature. This key projects a feeling of visual mood and atmosphere exactly the same way that a musical key projects an audible mood and atmosphere. The artist has discovered a visual mode that is perfectly attuned to the currents of our time.

His second area of originality is in the more formal functions of space and composition. Wesselmann achieves a spatial relationship in his collages that is new and personal. The result of the combination of these two areas of originality is a style that is as individual and distinctive as a fingerprint. This originality grew naturally out of Wesselmann's concern with the classic problems of art. His style can be traced in a direct line that runs through and connects the various periods of his work through the years.

In my paintings, I use the most traditional kind of situation—portraits, still life, nudes, and, more recently, landscapes. The specific subject materials are often determined by what is available to me. Billboards, bathrooms, and kitchens did not particularly excite me until I realized that they have a kind of superreality that could be exploited in painting. The real refrigerator in my kitchen does not excite me especially, but a refrigerator door that I can hold in my hands and walk around with and put into a painting does excite me. Billboards and commercial displays provide materials of extravagant quality and size, and I try to capitalize on this aspect in a particular painting.

The imagery in Wesselmann's collages is the result of a complex balance struck between the functional and abstract aspects of the elements used. Thus, a Wesselmann bathroom projects the undeniable feel and aura of a bathroom. A kitchen is unmistakably a kitchen. The individual elements are, however, transformed into integrated parts of the esthetic statement. A light fixture, for example, is treated as a mass that fills a specific area, whereas a shower curtain may become nothing more than a splash of color demanded by the compositional order of a particular piece.

> I try to make my work intense and exciting in a physical, rather than an emotional sense. I go to great lengths to avoid literary relationships arising from the juxtaposition of various elements. As a painter, I am not interested in social commentary, satire, or humor. I want the painting to rely on its own physical intensity and presence.

This attitude is allied to the integrity that is another important characteristic of Wesselmann's work. His craftsmanship is meticulous, and his compositions are carefully, painstakingly worked out. There is never anything shoddy or half-done in any of his completed work. Wesselmann respects honesty and work, and this respect is reflected in his art. Such simple, wholesome virtues have become unfashionable topics for discussion. Yet they are part of the man, and neither the artist nor his work can be adequately understood without considering them. They represent the epitome of the middle-class American ethic—a tradition in which Tom Wesselmann grew up.

He was the middle of three children born to a comfortable Cincinnati family. His father was and is an executive of a paper company. The family lived in a rambling brick-and-frame house that was part of a new residential street built on the outskirts of that most American of cities. A basketball court was set up in the backyard, and directly behind the house was a large tract of woodland. The family was closely knit and easy-going. Tom Wesselmann got along with an older brother and younger sister with no more than a normal amount of discord. His parents encouraged independence in their children and allowed them to make their own decisions.

If there was any torment in his life, it was superficial and internal, never the result of his environment. As a boy, Wesselmann felt no overwhelming ambition. It was assumed that he would go into business some day—either his father's or his own.

Anything as remotely Bohemian as art was completely alien to us. That kind of thing just did not exist in our world.

After graduation from high school, Tom Wesselmann enrolled in college. There was no serious ambition behind the move. Boys from his background were expected to go to college. Hiram College in Ohio was the school he chose.

I majored in psychology because I thought that this would be the easiest subject that I could develop any interest in. I was much more interested in sports at the time and played varsity basketball and golf.

As a student, young Wesselmann was indifferent, barely managing to make passing grades. He joined a fraternity; participated in the school's athletic programs; and showed little predilection for art, books, or ideas. His background was totally nonesthetic. He was committed to ordinary middle-class pursuits.

This comfortable semischolastic life was interrupted by the Army. Wesselmann was drafted—an experience that was to prove a turning-point in his life.

In the Army, I became seriously involved with something for the first time. Since high school, I had had a strong interest in humor. For years I collected and catalogued jokes and gags. The horror of Army life provoked me to create humor, purely in self-defense. This humor took the form of cartoons, and I began to teach myself how to draw.

After his discharge from the Army, Wesselmann returned to school. Although he had committed himself to a career in cartooning as a result of his Army experience, he felt that, since he had only one year to go, he might as well finish his studies and get his degree.

I was determined to become a cartoonist, and I figured that, with the GI Bill, I could afford to study for several years and hoped that this would give me enough time to really learn how to draw.

This ambition prompted Wesselmann to enroll at the Cincinnati Art Academy during his last year at college. Here he received his first formal training in art. A sympathetic teacher at the Art Academy suggested that Wesselmann apply to Cooper Union in New York. The school, he explained, was very good, and tuition was free. Wesselmann applied, took the entrance examination, and was accepted.

I enrolled at the school only because of my interest in cartooning. All I wanted from Cooper Union was time. I had no interest in art, and my ignorance was bliss. I had heard of Picasso, knew that there had been a Rembrandt, and was sure that Norman Rockwell was underrated. Art was a remote area that had nothing to do with my life.

At Cooper Union, however, courses in painting were among the required subjects. In these classes, Wesselmann first put brush to canvas. Painting was merely one of the things he had to do in order to remain at the school. He was still committed to cartooning, and all his energies were directed toward the mastery of drawing as it related to sight gags and cartoons.

In time, the creative atmosphere of the school and the city began to take effect. Wesselmann responded to this atmosphere, and his limited interests expanded. He discovered books and ideas and art. These discoveries, in turn, stimulated his interest in painting. Soon his painting classes became something more than technical requirements for remaining at school.

I slowly realized that I was no longer interested in cartooning. As my concern for painting went up, my involvement with cartooning went down. It was impossible for them to coexist. I could not walk around obsessed with seeing the world as material for humor and also be involved with painting. Nicholas Marsicano, one of my teachers at Cooper Union, was an important influence at the time. He introduced me to ideas about painting which excited me—especially the ideas of abstract expressionism. That revolution became personally significant to me, and I got caught up in its mystique. At some other time or in some other city, I doubt that I could have become interested in painting. As it was, it seemed completely hopeless because DeKooning had already painted all my paintings.

Toward the end of his final year at Cooper Union, Wesselmann abandoned his involvement with cartooning completely. Painting and collage became his primary concerns. He was fascinated by the textures of weathered objects, such as old newspapers, discarded rags, leaves, and worn package labels, and used them in his collages.

After graduation from Cooper Union, Wesselmann experienced a prolonged bout of depression, which had begun in the months prior to graduation. He was dissatisfied with his work and realized that he was now on his own. He felt that he was no more than an inept painter with an undefined interest in collage. Yet the urge to creation was there. Wesselmann doggedly continued to paint and work while supporting himself as a teacher in the New York school system—first in a Brooklyn junior high school and then at the High School of Art and Design in Manhattan.

Graduation and my depression forced me to abandon my student images, but I kept on with the general direction of what I felt a painting was. This change grew out of a realization that I was dishonest in trying to use DeKooning's wildness in my work. I had to find my own. It was partly a matter of accepting my own nature and trying to find something vital about it. I consoled myself by becoming aware of the peculiar wildness of Mondrian. My portrait collages began shortly after I went on my own. I felt the necessity to return to some kind of simple starting-point and to neutralize as many aspects of my painting as I could. Picasso, as Marsicano had said, invented all the shapes; Matisse had exhausted all the compositional devices. I tried to neutralize these aspects of painting about which I had become self-conscious as much as I could and started again from there.

It was during this period that the artist's approach to collage underwent a crucial change. Wesselmann became fascinated by the idea of the association of real objects within his compositions. Thus, a piece of wallpaper became a wall; a rug was the floor; sky became simply blue; grass, green. The elements in his collages stood for themselves—purely and simply.

He did a series of these small collages using paint together with objects and materials that represented themselves. For Wesselmann, this series was a revelation. Though the work was still clumsy and inept, it revealed a strength of imagery and composition that he had not seen in his work before. As Wesselmann continued working in this vein, he felt his control growing. Gradually, the craft became more polished, and the composition more authoritative. There was a development that could be measured from one piece to the next.

> In these early works I felt very arbitrary about color. But one night, after about a year of small nude collages, I had a dream about red, white, and blue. This dream provoked the "Great American Nude" series which provided an integrated set of arbitrary colors and shapes within which to limit myself.

The early collages in the "Great American Nude" series were small because Wesselmann felt that they had to be intimate. For a long time, the artist worked on a board which he held in his lap. As the series developed, however, Wesselmann discovered that the over-all feel of the collages was changing.

> I can only describe it as a tightening of the elements, a kind of process of depersonalization. Colors became flatter, cleaner, brighter; edges became harder, clearer; and there was more use of real objects —prints, bottles, advertisements, etc. The sound of the paintings became sharper. I felt the need to lock up my paintings so tightly that nothing could move. This way, by becoming static and somewhat anonymous, they also became more charged with energy.

These tendencies demanded an increase in size, and Wesselmann's canvases grew from small one-foot squares to four feet and more. The size of the collages was now determined by the size of the elements; the works became huge when the artist began using actual billboard images in his compositions.

Wesselmann had shown his early portrait collages and nudes at the Judson Gallery in Greenwich Village. His first exhibit of the "Great American Nude" series, however, was at the Tanager Gallery on East Tenth Street in late 1960. A year later, Wesselmann was invited to join the Green Gallery and had his first one-man show on Fifty-seventh

Street early in 1962. This exhibition established the artist in the fore-front of the new movement.

It was disturbing at first to hear about other painters whose work appeared to be related to mine. I had always felt cut off from the mainstream of the New York art world—like Rousseau in the midst of the cubists. This isolation was deliberate. I consciously attempted to work away from those around me. The big surprise was to discover that, in isolating myself, I wound up being closer to others than when I started.

Wesselmann lives in a combination studio and apartment in Greenwich Village. There is a large terrace behind the studio where a number of potted plants struggle to live. He is married to a gentle and beautiful girl who is sympathetic to the peculiar demands of the artist. He still enjoys fishing and golf whenever time permits.

Time is, however, at a premium. His work is demanding. In his studio, Wesselmann has a roomful of objects—billboards, displays, appliances, and other commercial images.

Each one represents a project that demands consideration. My main concern now is how to find the time to do all the things I want to do.

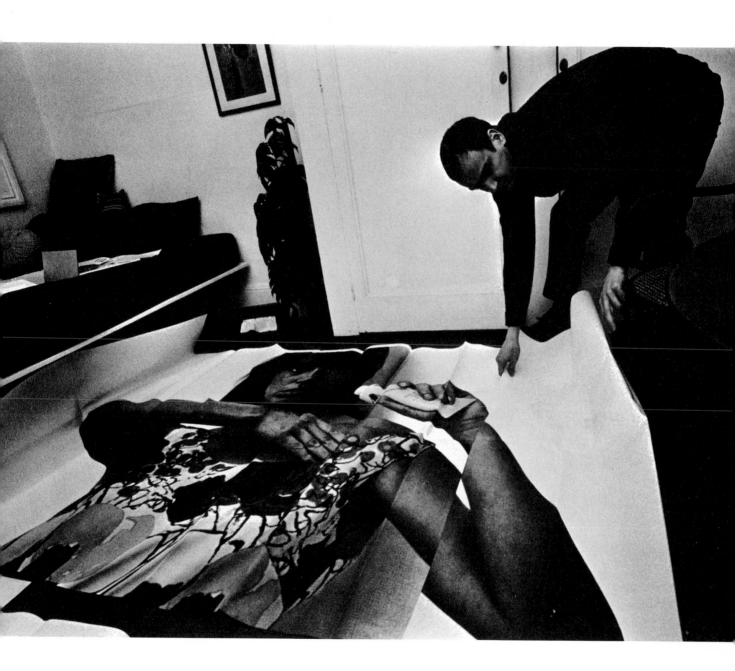

"Interior Number 1," Tom Wesselmann.
Collection Mr. and Mrs. Robert C. Scull.
Photograph: Eric Pollitzer.

(Right:) "Three-Dimensional Drawing
for Still Life Number 42,"
Tom Wesselmann.
Collection James Michener.
Photograph: Eric Pollitzer.

Claire Wesselmann

(*Below:*) "Bathtub Collage Number 3," Tom Wesselmann.
Courtesy Green Gallery, New York. Photograph: Rudolph Burckhardt.

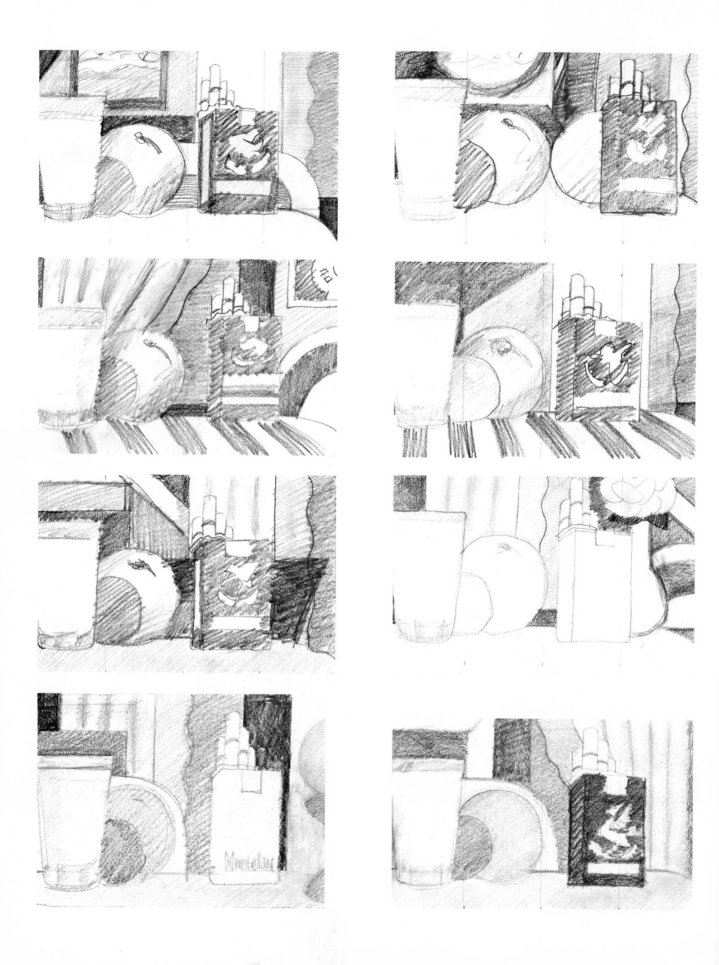

"Still Life Number 36," Tom Wesselmann.
Courtesy Green Gallery, New York.
Photograph: Rudolph Burckhardt.

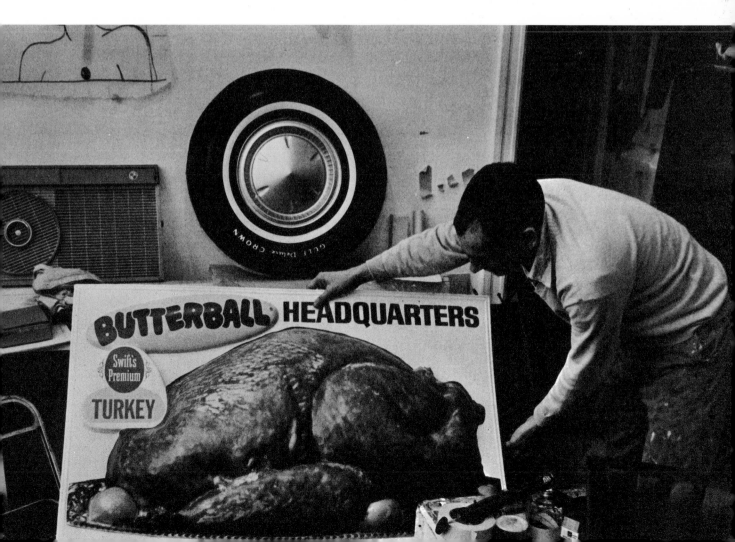

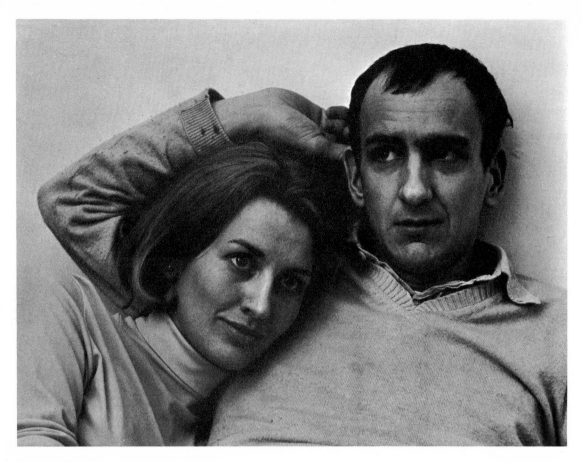

Claire and Tom Wesselmann

Stable Gallery, 1964

Collectors and Galleries

Art is a form of communication. Most artists want their work to be seen and appreciated—hopefully to the extent that others will pay for the privilege of owning it.

It is not an unreasonable desire. Before he can begin to consider himself a master of his craft, the artist must undergo a long period of schooling and another long period of apprenticeship. He has every right to expect appreciation and adequate recompense for his labors. Yet the creation of the artist is, at best, a most tenuous commodity. Through the splash of color on a flat plane of canvas or through form imposed on stone or bronze, the artist attempts to create beauty, and beauty cannot be sold like a loaf of bread on a grocery shelf.

No one is more aware of this contradiction than the artist. He, more so than any other professional, is prepared to accept obscurity and neglect. As one artist remarked, shrugging philosophically at a loft full of his unsold paintings: "Nobody asked me to paint them."

Historically, the artist—and especially the artist who is also a radical innovator—has had a hard time of it. The garret has been his traditional realm and poverty his handmaiden. Cézanne sold few paintings in his lifetime, and van Gogh's tribulations have been celebrated endlessly. In our own time, we have the example of Jackson Pollock, who was plagued by financial difficulties long after he had realized the most important artistic innovation in fifty years.

With the pop movement, however, a precedent has been established. The artists who created this school, and all of them are innovators of the most radical order, have enjoyed recognition and financial reward in a remarkably short time—so short, in fact, that their success is looked on as a phenomenon in the art world. And this phenomenon is even more remarkable in that it was accomplished in the face of almost universal critical condemnation and the marked antagonism of the established powers of the art world. The "modern" museums are only now beginning to accept the esthetic premises of the movement.

The responsibility for this happy precedent must be assumed by a small group of intrepid and daring collectors. It takes neither imagination nor great esthetic sensibility to purchase a Rembrandt; all it takes is a lot of loot. And even then the purchase is more in the nature of a gilt-edged investment. To buy a painting that has been critically reviled and that friends, neighbors, and even one's wife will most likely laugh at, however, takes a large measure of both qualities plus a generous dose of independence.

Probably the most influential collector in this rare group is Robert C. Scull, a New York City taxicab and insurance magnate. Scull was one of the first to recognize the esthetic significance of the movement and has followed the school from its inception. His collection provides a panoramic history of the group.

The paintings that hang in his Fifth Avenue apartment trace a development that leads directly from a Jasper Johns beer can to the full-blown pop expression of a Roy Lichtenstein comic-strip panel. Scull's Oldenburgs, Rosenquists, Warhols, and Wesselmanns live happily and in perfect harmony with his Klines, DeKoonings, Rothkos, Stills, and a superb collection of antique furniture and Renaissance bronzes.

His patronage has been directly responsible for at least one of the pioneer galleries that exhibited works of the pop artists. The organization of the Green Gallery, which first showed the pop works of Oldenburg, Rosenquist, and Wesselmann, was made possible to a large degree by Scull's promise to purchase a certain amount of work from the gallery during its initial years. This agreement provided the financial basis without which Richard Bellamy, owner and director, would have found it difficult to open the gallery.

> The art of any society is its most lasting and meaningful accomplishment. Here in the pop-art movement we have a perfect expression of our world. The artists who have created this movement are a glory—to America and the world. I, for one, am grateful to them for the beauty they have created—beauty that enriches my life.

Oddly enough, one of the first pop-art collectors was a European

—the Italian industrialist Count Giuseppe Panza di Biumo, with homes in Milan and Varese. Panza has been an admirer of American art since he began collecting such abstract expressionists as Rothko and Kline. He was in New York early in 1962, where he saw the pop-art exhibits of Rosenquist, Lichtenstein, and Oldenburg. His reaction was immediate. He bought the works of these artists en masse and shipped them home to Italy. Today, the Villa Panza, built in the grand manner on a hill overlooking Varese in 1750, is adorned with such blatantly American images as Rosenquist billboard paintings, Lichtenstein comic strips, Rauschenberg combines, and Oldenburg hamburgers. Panza himself remains a staunch supporter of the new school, keeping in close touch with latest developments.

Richard Brown-Baker is one of this band of early pop art collectors. Brown-Baker is the happy possessor of a modest private income and an immodest commitment to art who has developed a remarkably perceptive and prophetic eye. Not only has he been an early collector of pop art, but he was also an early collector of abstract expressionism and of the still-developing school of hard-edged geometric abstractionism.

> I leave the established artists to others. My principal joy in collecting lies in the discovery of new, unrecognized talents. It gives me great satisfaction to watch unknown young artists grow and develop.

The fruits of Brown-Baker's perceptive eye are evident in his spacious West Side apartment—its spaciousness dwarfed by his collection. One room, for example, contains a wall-to-wall arrangement of stacks that bulge with paintings. In the rest of the apartment, wall space has practically disappeared under a blanket of art.

> The pop school is as exciting and vital as any of the other movements that have characterized the history of art. Like every important school, it breaks new ground, extending the existing esthetic limits by offering us a new perspective on the world in which we live.

Leon Manuchin, a corporation lawyer, is another member of the group. A man with a sophisticated sense of humor and an encyclopedic knowledge of modern art, Manuchin has been a lifelong student and appreciator of art. He began collecting in the 1930's, when he acquired works by artists of the social-realist school.

Over the years, however, his tastes enlarged to include the cubists, postimpressionists, abstract expressionists, and now pop artists. Manuchin's Park Avenue apartment provides an elegant backdrop for his collection. Among the pieces he owns is a Lichtenstein comic-strip rendering of a Picasso painting. He also owns an original Picasso work of a similar style. The two paintings provide a capsule history of the development of art during the years that separated their respective creations.

> I enjoy pop art. I like the humanity in the work and the humor with which these artists depict our world. They have given us a new way of looking at everyday objects, revealing facets and beauty that we never suspected before.

Leon Kraushar, an insurance broker, is also an important pop-art collector. Unlike the others mentioned, however, he was not among the earliest collectors. He discovered the school after it had become fairly well established. His unstinting enthusiasm for the work of the pop artists has, however, helped him make up for lost time and has enabled him to amass the largest and most important private collection. His strikingly contemporary home in Lawrence, Long Island, has been transformed into a kind of temple of pop art. The works of artists from this school cover the walls of every room.

> My wife introduced me to art. About five years ago we began collecting—mostly French postimpressionist and other European works. I was never particularly sympathetic to these paintings. I found the preciousness of the image stale. The paintings did, however, stimulate my interest in art. It was when I discovered pop art that I became really involved. Here was a timely and aggressive image that spoke directly to me about things I understood. The paintings from this school are today. The expression is completely American, with no apologies to the European past. This is my art, the only work being done today that has meaning for me.

There are, of course, many more collectors besides the handful mentioned here. Space, however, limits the number we can deal with adequately.

At least as important as the collectors in the spectacular success of pop art were the galleries that first showed the works of this movement. The Leo Castelli Gallery, for example, played a crucial role in the promotion of the school. By exhibiting the works of Roy Lichtenstein, the gallery helped introduce the movement to the public.

The Castelli Gallery was prepared to accept pop art because of its involvement with Jasper Johns and Robert Rauschenberg. These two artists represent a bridge between the "sensibilities" painters associated with the abstract-expressionist experience and the fundamentally antisensibility art of the pop movement. Between the exhibition of a Jasper Johns flag or a Robert Rauschenberg combine and the showing of a Roy Lichtenstein comic-strip painting there is no great esthetic step. The work of these artists is related, and thus the Castelli Gallery was both esthetically and psychologically ready to accept the innovation posed by the art of Lichtenstein.

The Green Gallery, directed by Richard Bellamy, played an equally important role in the development of the pop movement. Bellamy is an astute student of art with an enthusiastic and perceptive eye for nuances of expression. He recognized the validity of the pop esthetic immediately, and his response took the very practical form of swift advocacy.

Bellamy committed the resources of his newly organized gallery wholeheartedly to the movement and gave the artists his unstinting support. The pop works of Oldenburg, Rosenquist, and Wesselmann were exhibited at the Green Gallery, and the excitement generated by these exhibits was to an important degree responsible for the establishment of the movement.

Then there is the Stable Gallery, directed by Eleanor Ward, which first showed the Campbell Soup cans and Marilyn Monroes that brought notoriety to Andy Warhol. This gallery also exhibited the works of Robert Indiana and Marisol Escobar, both closely related to the pop movement. These three galleries—Leo Castelli, Green, and Stable—introduced pop art.

An additional impetus was given the movement when the Sidney Janis Gallery, which was an early champion of the abstract expressionists, organized a comprehensive exhibit of the school early in 1963. This was the most ambitious group show assembled up to that time and created a great deal of excitement. This exhibit succeeded in establishing the pop school as an important contribution to the vigorous stream of American art.

Since the early days of the movement, there has been considerable shifting of artists and galleries. Rosenquist and Warhol, for example, are now associated with the Castelli Gallery, and Oldenburg has joined Sidney Janis. And there will be more shifts in the future.

Primarily, however, the school was and is a collectors' movement. Collectors were the principal champions of the group, and they are responsible for the success of the school. In this instance, the collectors led the way. It is ironic that an art based directly on the most common images of our world should appeal to the most sophisticated tastes. Irony is, however, very much a part of our world—a world that pop art expresses so eloquently.

24 GIANT SIZE PKGS.
New!
Brillo®
soap pads
WITH RUST RESISTER
SHINES ALUMINUM FAST

Ethel Scull with portrait by Andy Warhol

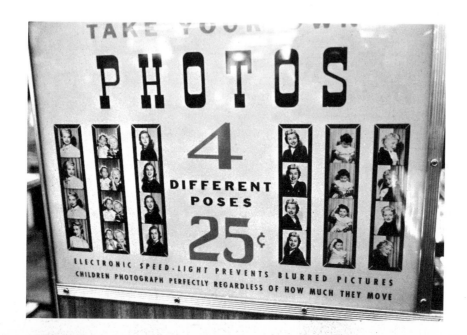

obert C. Scull

Dining room, Robert C. Scull home

View, Richard Brown-Baker home

View, Leon Manuchin home

Views, Leon Kraushar home

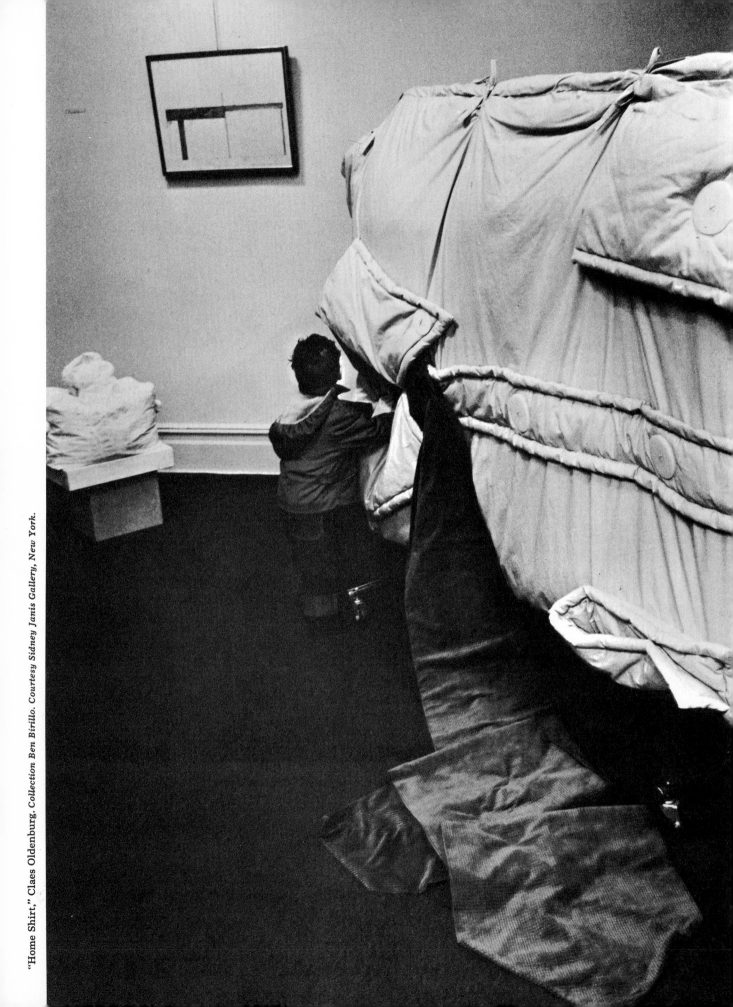

"Roma," Mel Ramos.
Collection Ben Birillo.

The New Wave

Anyone who has been exposed to pop art on something more than the most superficial level is compelled to see the world around him in a new perspective. His reactions to that world may not be altered to any great extent, but its reality becomes heightened, amplified. Our gaudy landscape of blatant commercial imagery is brought into sharper focus than ever before, and the world becomes a never-ending spectacle of pop art. In this instance, the artist serves the function ascribed to him by Nietzsche: he makes palatable those aspects of the world that are most nauseating.

It is in the realm of art, however, that the most significant influence of pop art has been felt. There is hardly an artist working in America today—indeed, in the world—who is not aware of the innovations engendered by the movement and has not reacted to them. This reaction takes many forms. Scores of pop artists have emerged in America, Europe, and even Asia. The bulk of their work, like the bulk of most human endeavor, is mediocre, with one important difference: when pop art is mediocre, it is terrible.

The esthetic of the school is subtle and so demanding of the selectivity and sensitivity of the artist that only the most authentic and highly developed talents can make its creation work. Pop art, in dealing with the most common and ordinary images of our world, leads the casual creator into a trap. The thematic sources are so obvious and blatant that they lull the critical faculties.

Working in this idiom, the artist is precariously poised on the edge of artistic disaster. He must explore the expressive potentialities of the vulgar and banal, but his creation can be neither. He must exploit these qualities without evoking them. The ability to strike this balance is rare, but the temptation to try is great. It is a challenge that artists apparently find difficult to resist. The result is a flood of pop art that threatens to engulf the originators. Fortunately, enough artists of ability appear out of this creative surge to assure the continued development of the movement.

Allan D'Arcangelo., best known for his stark and startling depictions of the American highway, for example, has already made an important addition to the school. By utilizing the imagery of pop art in combination with a personal surrealist sense, D'Arcangelo has developed an individual style.

His exploration of the highway as a symbolic thematic source culminated in a commission to create a large mural at the Transportation Building at the New York World's Fair. This mural, which has been seen by millions of visitors, is a superb evocation of a vital aspect of our world. By exploiting the specialized vocabulary of the pop esthetic in a sensitive and imaginative manner, D'Arcangelo has created a work of visual strength and immediate appeal. Although his imagery can be considered crass and blatant, the mural stands as an important contemporary statement. The imagery is perfectly adapted to express this particular aspect of reality.

Working in an entirely different vein is Richard Artschwager, a carpenter by trade, who, appropriately enough, makes furniture. His furniture is, however, not the kind you sit on or find in the average home. Actually, Artschwager makes sculpture of wood and Formica.

Cold, utterly mechanical, and devoid of all personality, Artschwager's creations are idealized versions of functional contemporary furniture. Their presence is evocative of Bauhaus—but Bauhaus as it has been modified in the process of commercial design for mass-produced articles. In Artschwager's hands, however, this aspect is heightened and transformed in a peculiarly disturbing expression.

The Formica used in his creations, for example, is insensitive. He has sought out obvious and inane colors and patterns and has contrasted these qualities with the classic, functional simplicity of the lines utilized in his work. The reality of both aspects is thus heightened with the completed image suspended between the tensions generated by the two extremes.

In Artschwager's statement, the pop-art influence is more subtle than it is in D'Arcangelo's. It is in evidence, however, in the choice of materials and in the thematic sources. Artschwager's art shares the same concern with the common image and exploits the visual appeal and psychological presence of the overly familiar.

Mel Ramos, a young painter from Los Angeles, belongs to this growing group of promising new pop artists. He imposes an elegant painting technique on a startling choice of subject matter. Like Lichtenstein, Ramos paints comic-strip characters. But, whereas Lichtenstein renders them in the comic-strip style, Ramos paints them in the grand manner.

Batman, Superman, the Sandman—all familiar comic-strip heroes —are among his subjects. His favorite theme on which he has extended his best efforts is, however, the voluptuous, sexy heroine typical of the "girlie" comic book that combines the appeal of scantily clad girls with traditional comic-strip rendering to win its adherents. These heroines, in suggestive, often perverse costumes, provide a fruitful theme for the artist. By eliminating sensitivity from his stark depictions of these lusty ladies, Ramos exaggerates the cheapness and vulgarity of his models. This very exaggeration, however, rescues the image from all vestiges of vulgarity. The subject is transformed. She becomes an idealization of a particularly heady type of feminine appeal.

In his best efforts, Ramos achieves an honesty and ruthlessness of image that compels attention. Although his subject matter has been influenced directly by the pop movement, he has exploited the premise of the school by adapting it to his own creative directions. He has expressed his individuality in terms of the pop experience.

Robert Stanley, a native New Yorker, is a young artist who also exploits the techniques of pop art in a markedly individual way. In his paintings, Stanley reduces the subject to distinct areas of light and dark that are then painted in optically activating colors. The image, though abstracted, remains clearly recognizable.

Combining the visual excitement of "optical painting" with the elegant formality of hard-edged abstraction, Stanley's work fits into the pop fold by virtue of the imagery. Using this technique, he paints rock-and-roll singers—groups and individuals—sports figures, surfboard enthusiasts, erotica, and other popularly celebrated scenes and personalities. These paintings, which exploit the visual effects of various schools and movements, generate their own peculiar intensity that reacts with the subject matter to project a highly individual, exciting statement.

An entirely different line of investigation within the pop mystique has been initiated by Robert Watts, an art instructor at Rutgers University. Watts, who has been involved with the pop movement since its inception, is a proponent of manufactured art, of an expression dependent solely on the selectivity of the artist, in that the rendering is accomplished through industrial processes.

Following this line of investigation, Watts has created a comprehensive body of transformed objects: chrome-plated cabbages and cauliflowers, lead confections, bronzed eggs, flocked bananas, hot dogs wrapped in patriotic bunting, ceramic breads, and, most recently, three cases of tomatoes rendered in moribund shades of white, gray, and black wax—the ultimate in processed food.

In these creations, the depersonalization of art inadvertently begun by Jasper Johns and Robert Rauschenberg becomes complete. By subjecting real objects to a mechanical process of plating or coating, Watts emphasizes both their functional and esthetic qualities. The transformation lends these objects an importance that is not apparent in their untreated states. Evoking a puckish humor, Watts has also created edible art. Utilizing the decorative techniques of the baker, he has made fanciful pop-art cakes. Here is the last word in functional art; you not only look at Watts's cakes, but you can also eat them.

Another artist who has broken new ground within the pop esthetic is Gerald Foyster, an ex-industrial designer whose investigation centers on an optical gimmick. Foyster utilizes a commercially developed novelty which creates an illusion of animation through the viewing of separate, synchronized images as the eye moves across an optical grate which focuses on a different image at various angles of view.

His statement is related to that of the school of retinal painters who explore the vibrant qualities of such colors as red and blue when they are placed beside each other. The close juxtaposition of such colors acts on the retina to create an illusion of movement. In Foyster's case, however, the illusion is fully realized. Depth and motion are actually achieved, whereas in ordinary retinal painting it is merely approached.

The optical material used in Foyster's creations is manufactured. The artist simply arranges it in more or less formal compositions. Here is manufactured art with a minimum of artistic manipulation. The material, commercially manufactured and distributed, is used as an end in itself. Yet, as exploited by Gerald Foyster, this material lends itself to a valid esthetic statement. The creations of the artist have presence and a distinctly individual aura. And why not? Is this not exactly what all art does—impose a more or less formal composition on familiar materials? Artists have traditionally used paint or stone or bronze. Foyster uses an optical toy. One is no less permissible or valid than the other.

Foyster's creations take their esthetic from a manufactured novelty with little or no individual transformation. Thus, the artist's function becomes both absolute and negligible. Art is, in this case, created solely through the selectivity of the artist. Technique, craft, sensibility become extraneous. For all practical purposes, the line that separates art and life disappears.

It is a bold innovation, but one that falls within the premise of the pop esthetic. And the works themselves are a delight. Bright and festive, they beguile the eye with their quick animation and immediate appeal. Gerald Foyster discovered a unique medium in an optical toy that he utilizes in the creation of a new kind of art.

There are, of course, many other artists who have responded to the innovations of pop art. It would be impossible to list them all. Indeed, pop artists—good, bad, and indifferent—emerge daily. A new area of investigation with unlimited expressive possibilities has been opened. Its ramifications will be felt for years to come.

The influence of pop art is not limited to artists, however. The movement has also affected the traditional gallery exhibit. In the past, a one-man show was a comparatively simple affair. The most recent works of an artist were gathered and hung to advantage, and the show was opened to the public. It is an efficient method and will certainly be continued in the future.

Pop art, however, demands something more. Derivative, as it is, from the world around us, it needs a more comprehensive approach for effective presentation. Most of the artists associated with the movement have felt a certain lack in traditional exhibitions. Claes Oldenburg, for example, has always thought of his one-man shows as the creation of a total environment. This concept was evident in his "Store" exhibition, which was arranged as a store in an ordinary Lower East Side storefront. His "Bedroom," which was shown in a group exhibit at the Sidney Janis Gallery, was another step in this direction.

This line of development was exploited by the Bianchini Gallery, which opened the 1964 season with a group show entitled "The American Supermarket." Conceived and organized by Ben Birillo, an artist who has been close to the pop movement since it began, it represents an exciting new concept in gallery exhibitions. A group of artists combined their efforts in the creation of an integrated environment based on a single theme. In this case, the gallery itself was arranged to resemble a supermarket, with aisles, cases, banked shelves, and even a check-out counter. Working within this framework, the artists contributed their individual efforts.

James Rosenquist contributed a "Noxzema $100,000 Be-Beautiful Contest" painting; Roy Lichtenstein made a series of enameled hot-dog displays; Tom Wesselmann created a still life depicting a freshly roasted turkey; Andy Warhol signed and arranged a pyramid of Campbell Soup cans, as well as a stack of supermarket cartons and silk-screened shopping bags; Robert Watts was put in charge of vegetables and fruits, which he chromeplated for the occasion; Claes Oldenburg was represented by a jar of pickles, a slice of pie, and a candy-bar display; Jasper Johns's beer cans, created in 1959 as one of the first expressions of pop art, dominated the beverage department; Richard Artschwager made the check-out counter; Mary Inman provided wax replicas of meat, cheese, fish, fowl, and bread; and Billy Apple painted a series of Apple paintings to complete the supermarket. Soothing and meaningless Muzak-type harmonies were piped through a sound system, interrupted now and then by an announcer intoning unadvertised specials.

This exciting exhibition was just one manifestation of the continuing vitality of the pop movement. More will surely be revealed in the future. The school is young, still in its inception, and it is impossible to predict its course. All we can say for certain is that pop art has arrived, and the world will never be the same again.

"Stamp Vendor," Robert Watts

"Road Series Number 13," Allan D'Arcangelo.
Courtesy Fischbach Gallery, New York.
Photograph: Eric Pollitzer.

"Mick ('Rolling Stones')," Bob Stanley.
Collection William S. Zierler.
Photograph: Walter Rosenbaum.

"Tract Home," Richard Artschwager.
Courtesy Leo Castelli Gallery, New York.
Photograph: Rudolph Burckhardt.

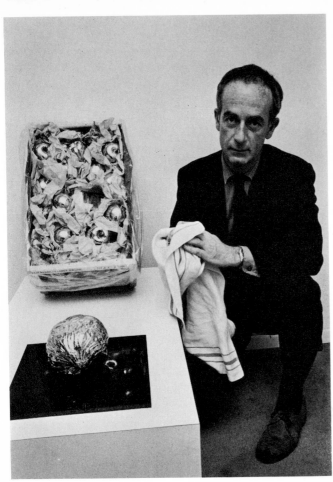

Robert Watts

Gerald Foyster

Ben Birillo

Ivan Karp

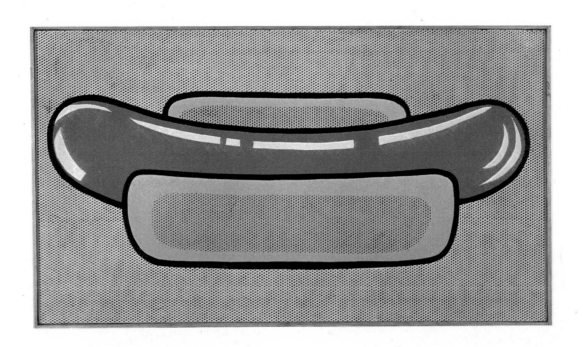

"Hot Dog," 1962
24 × 36"
ROY LICHTENSTEIN
Private collection, Paris
Courtesy Ileana Sonnabend Gallery, Paris

"Nurse," 1964
40 × 40"
ROY LICHTENSTEIN
Collection Leon Kraushar

"Portrait of Allan Kaprow," 1962
20 × 24"
ROY LICHTENSTEIN
Collection Irving Beck

"Portrait of Ivan Karp," 1962
20 × 24"
ROY LICHTENSTEIN
Collection Irving Beck

"Eddie," 1962
30 × 45" diptych
ROY LICHTENSTEIN
Courtesy Ileana Sonnabend Gallery, Paris

"Two Swimmers," 1963
72 × 96"
ROY LICHTENSTEIN
Collection Leon Kraushar

"Landscape," 1964
34 × 60"
ROY LICHTENSTEIN
Collection Leon Kraushar

"Stove with Meats," 1961
Life size
CLAES OLDENBURG
Collection Mr. and Mrs. Robert C. Scull

"Hamburger with Pickle and Olive," 1963
Life size
CLAES OLDENBURG
Collection Giuseppe Panza, Milan
Courtesy Ileuna Sonnabend Gallery, Paris

"Bacon and Eggs," 1962
Approximately 30 × 50″
CLAES OLDENBURG
Collection Leon Kraushar

"Pastry Case," 1961
Life size
CLAES OLDENBURG
Courtesy Sidney Janis Gallery, New York

"Bedroom," 1964
CLAES OLDENBURG with PAT OLDENBURG
Installation, Sidney Janis Gallery, New York

"Green Stockings," 1962
Approximately 30 × 48″
CLAES OLDENBURG
Collection Mr. and Mrs. Robert C. Scull

"The Store," 1963
CLAES OLDENBURG
Installation, Green Gallery, New York

"The Home," 1964
CLAES OLDENBURG
Installation, Sidney Janis Gallery, New York

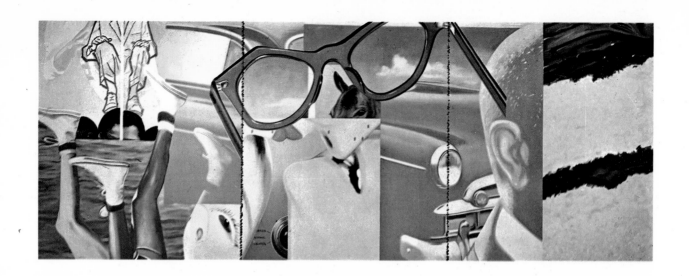

"For the American Negro," 1963
6½ × 15½'
JAMES ROSENQUIST
Courtesy Green Gallery, New York

"Rainbow," 1962
50 × 62"
JAMES ROSENQUIST
Courtesy Ileana Sonnabend Gallery, Paris

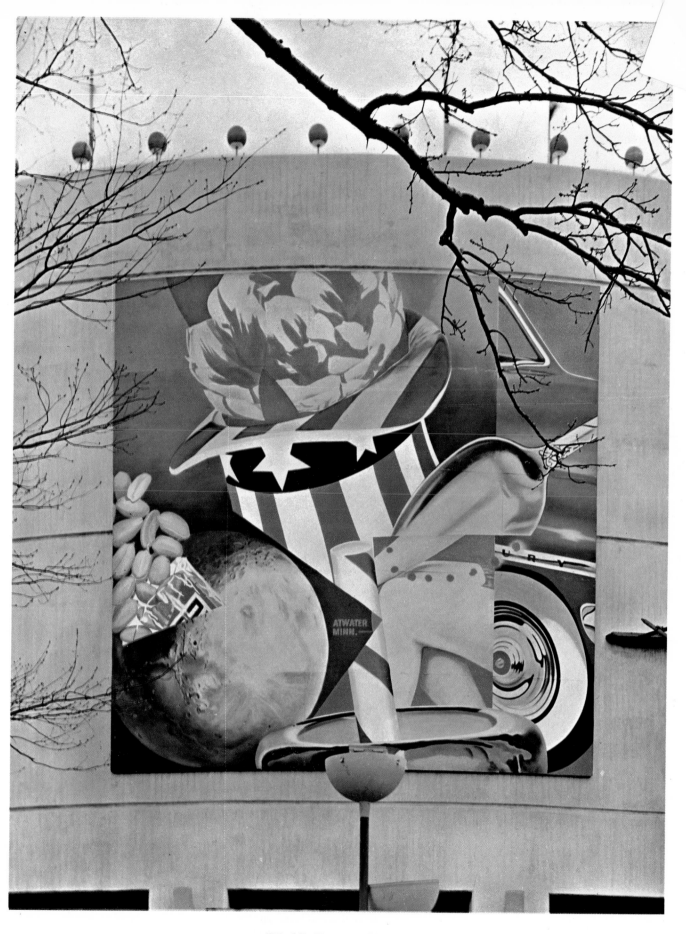

"World's Fair Mural," 1964
8 × 20′
JAMES ROSENQUIST
Courtesy Leo Castelli Gallery, New York

"Silo," 1964
8½ × 12 × 2′
JAMES ROSENQUIST
Courtesy Leo Castelli Gallery, New York

"Dishes," 1964
50 × 60″
JAMES ROSENQUIST
Courtesy Leo Castelli Gallery, New York

"Brillo Boxes," 1964
Life size
ANDY WARHOL
Collection Leon Kraushar

"Campbell Soup Can 19¢," 1962
16 × 20"
ANDY WARHOL
Collection Pasadena Art Museum

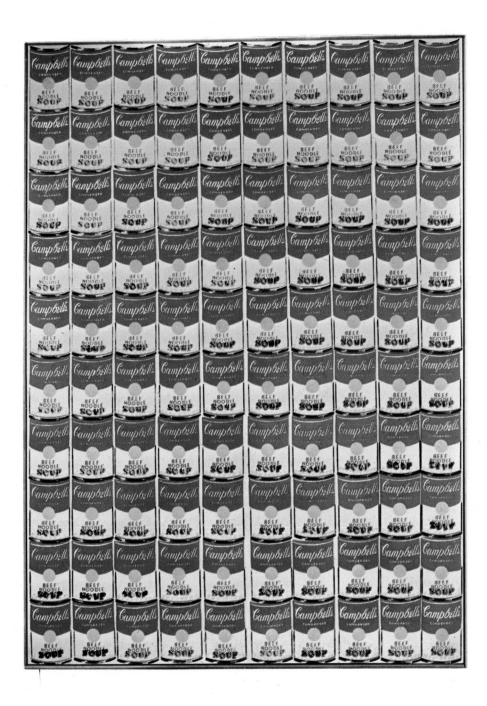

"One Hundred Campbell Soup Cans," 1962
52 × 82"
ANDY WARHOL
Collection Leon Kraushar

"Elizabeth Taylor," 1963
40 × 40"
ANDY WARHOL
Collection Leon Kraushar

"Marilyn Monroe," 1964
40 × 40"
ANDY WARHOL
Collection Leon Kraushar

"Landscape Number 2," 1964
6'3" × 7'10" × 3"
TOM WESSELMANN
Courtesy Green Gallery, New York

"Great American Nude Number 48," 1963
7 × 9 × 3'
TOM WESSELMANN
Collection Frederick Weisman
Courtesy Green Gallery, New York

"Bathtub Collage Number 1," 1963
4' × 5' × 4"
TOM WESSELMANN
Collection Leon Kraushar

"Great American Nude Number 51," 1963
10 × 12'
TOM WESSELMANN
Courtesy Green Gallery, New York

"Great American Nude Number 30," 1962
48 × 60"
TOM WESSELMANN
Collection Mr. and Mrs. Robert C. Scull

"Buffalo II," 1964
48 × 60″
ROBERT RAUSCHENBERG
Courtesy Leo Castelli Gallery, New York

"Savarin Can with Brushes," 1960
Life size
JASPER JOHNS
Collection of the artist

"Device Circle," 1960
36 × 48"
JASPER JOHNS
Collection Mr. and Mrs. Burton Tremaine, Meriden, Conn.

"Tie Tie," 1961
48 × 48″
JAMES DINE
Courtesy Sidney Janis Gallery, New York

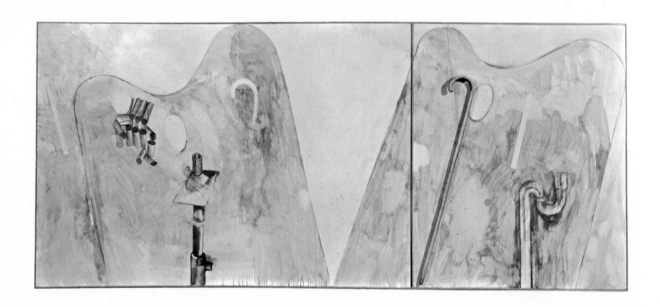

"Two Palettes," 1963
48 × 72″
JAMES DINE
Courtesy Sidney Janis Gallery, New York

"Meat Case," 1964
Life size
MARY INMAN
Collection Leon Kraushar

"The Supermarket," 1964
Installation, Bianchini Gallery, New York

"Chrome Fruits and Vegetables," 1964
Life Size
ROBERT WATTS
Courtesy Bianchini Gallery, New York

"Campbell Soup Can Pyramid," 1964
ANDY WARHOL
Installation, Bianchini Gallery, New York

"Campbell Soup Can on Shopping Bag," 1964
Life size
ANDY WARHOL
Courtesy Bianchini Gallery, New York

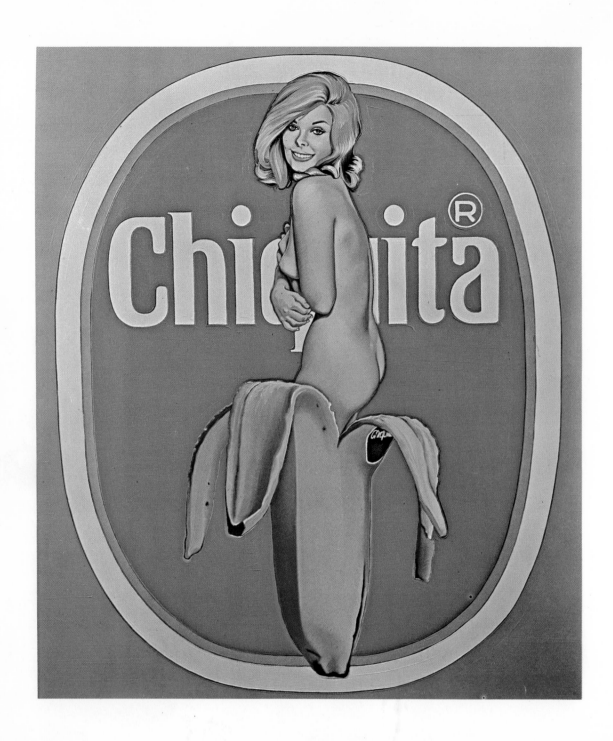

"Chiquita Banana," 1964
72 × 72"
MEL RAMOS
Collection Irving Beck
Courtesy Bianchini Gallery, New York

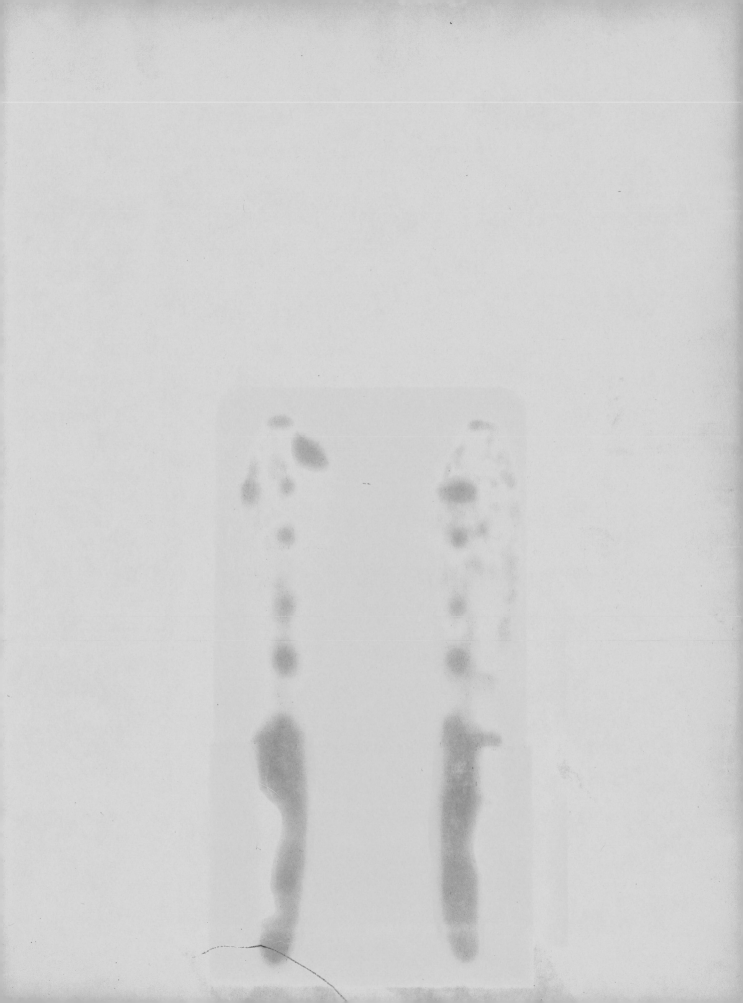

10/13/66